THE ACTIVIST ADVOCATE

THE ACTIVIST ADVOCATE

Policy Making in State Supreme Courts

Charles S. Lopeman

Westport, Connecticut
London

Library of Congress Cataloging-in-Publication Data

Lopeman, Charles S.
  The activist advocate : policy making in state supreme courts /
Charles S. Lopeman.
    p.   cm.
  Includes bibliographical references and index.
  ISBN 0–275–96455–8 (alk. paper)
  1. Courts of last resort—United States—States. 2. Judicial
review—United States—States. 3. Political questions and judicial
power—United States—States. I. Title.
KF8736.L67   1999
347.73′26—dc21   99–21597

British Library Cataloguing in Publication Data is available.

Library of Congress Catalog Card Number: 99–21597
ISBN: 0–275–96455–8

First published in 1999

Praeger Publishers, 88 Post Road West, Westport, CT 06881
An imprint of Greenwood Publishing Group, Inc.
www.praeger.com

Printed in the United States of America

The paper used in this book complies with the
Permanent Paper Standard issued by the National
Information Standards Organization (Z39.48–1984).

10 9 8 7 6 5 4 3 2 1

To my mother
    . . . a friend indeed.

Contents

Preface

For much of this century most state supreme courts have taken a back seat in establishing and changing policy for their states. They regularly agreed with the policy embedded in the laws adopted by their states' legislatures. They affirmed the policy that earlier courts had developed and that had become the doctrine of their states' common law. When an unusual case presented a unique problem that existing policy did not answer or answered unsatisfactorily, the state supreme courts looked to their legislatures to come up with a solution.

Although the state supreme courts occupied a secondary policy-making role to their legislatures, after the mid-1930s these legislatures occupied a significantly reduced role in public policy making as the Congress expanded the scope and reach of its powers beyond the restrictions of the dual federalism accommodation. At about the same time the U.S. Supreme Court became active in the enforcement of the rights and liberties guaranteed by the U.S. Constitution and the state supreme courts fell in line and accepted these interpretations by the U.S. Supreme Court as policy for their states. This inferior policy-making role of the states was changed during the 1980s. Calls by forces of various political allegiance for the devolution of power and responsibility from the Congress resulted in congressional invitation to the states to become active in designing the rules that govern their citizens. This devolution continued and increased in scope during the 1990s. The U.S. Supreme Court invited the state supreme courts to become independent policy makers by the use of their *state* constitutions. The courts in some states began, after World War II, to critically examine their common-law doctrine in the area of tort law. When they realized that their state's common law provided protections that were out of step with the times, these courts began to change the common-law doctrine. These and some other state supreme courts accepted the suggestion of the U.S. Supreme Court to become independent and began to use their state constitutions' protections. Not all state supreme courts have reexamined the policy of their states' common law nor have all chosen to give independent interpretation to their states' constitutions. The state supreme courts that have, have became important policy makers in their states. There has been no explanation why some state supreme courts choose to be policy makers in their states while others decline their opportunities. At this juncture of the devolution of policy-making authority from the Congress to the states and invitation to the state supreme courts by the U.S. Supreme Court to make independent policy on the basis of state constitutions, I hope that this book will illuminate the increasingly important decision by state supreme court that results in participation or avoidance of state-level policy making.

Acknowledgments

The idea for this study of judicial activism in state supreme courts resulted from the work that Larry Baum has done in the area of judicial activism and in state politics generally. My understanding of judicial decision making has benefited immeasurably from his study and my interest was aroused by his belief that state courts have been under-studied. I hasten to clarify that Professor Baum does not necessarily agree with the premises on which this book is based or the conclusions I reach herein.

I have been encouraged and supported in my efforts to write this book by the Political Science Department of the State University of West Georgia and particularly by its Chair, Janet Clark. It would have been impossible to have completed it without this support. I cannot thank Anita Immele, Department Secretary, and Amy Goolsby, Student Assistant, enough for the technical assistance they unhesitatingly provided during those times when I "made no tracks in the sand."

Donadrian Rice, Chair of the Psychology Department of the State University of West Georgia, guided me to research in his field that was relevant to my purposes. He was generous with his time and knowledge, but bears no responsibility for the application I made of the works to which he guided me.

Finally, I am deeply indebted to Larry Baum and Eric Waltenburg who read an earlier draft of the first chapter and each made very helpful suggestions that improved that chapter as well as the book. This is not meant to imply that either agrees with the premises on which this book is based or on the conclusions that I have reached in it. They generously reacted to the framework I had established and their suggestions improved the final result substantially. Any errors in concept or presentation are mine alone.

Chapter 1

Judicial Policy Making: An Overview

Until recently, victims of drunken drivers in Indiana could not sue the bar owners who sold a drunk the drinks, even if the owners had known that their customer was drunk. Neither the Indiana legislature nor the Indiana Supreme Court had previously created the right of injured persons to sue the bar for their injuries. The Indiana Supreme Court intentionally and actively made Indiana policy when it created a new cause of action for the injured victim.[1] The West Virginia legislature had created local school districts and provided that the public schools within these districts would be supported by local property taxes. The West Virginia Supreme Court disagreed with the legislature's system of support and required it to abandon local funding for public schools and provide for equal funding for all state school districts, rich or poor.[2] In Ohio, the common-law doctrine of family immunity that had been established by earlier Ohio courts required that families had to control whether and on what condition a person who has been injured by another may bear the costs of accidental injuries caused by one family member to another. The Ohio Supreme Court shifted these costs to insurance companies by overruling long established doctrine that had prevented injured children from suing their parents[3] and injured husbands and wives from suing their spouses.[4]

Obviously, the Indiana Supreme Court made public policy when, instead of waiting for the Indiana legislature to act, it established by its decision a right to sue bar owners who sell alcoholic beverages to intoxicated customers. When the West Virginia Supreme Court disagreed with its legislature in the school finance cases, it intentionally made public policy. It examined the legislature's policy and substituted for it the court's own preferred policies. Not all state policy has initially been made by state legislatures; some has been prescribed in decisions made by state courts at an earlier time. Common-law tort doctrines are examples of court-made policy. They are rules that sue for the value of the damage. The Ohio Supreme Court substituted its own preferred policy and made it possible for victims of intrafamily harm to bring suits for the resulting damage. When a court effectively disagrees with these earlier-made rules and substitutes its own, it makes policy, just as it does when it changes the policy made by the legislature. When the

Ohio Supreme Court overruled established common-law doctrine, it was clearly disagreeing with a policy of an earlier court. It was also, inferentially, disagreeing with the state legislature because the legislature had the power to change the judicially established common-law rules.

The Indiana, West Virginia, and Ohio courts were important policy makers in their states.[5] The courts in some other states declined similar opportunities to establish their states' policy. The Florida court would not recognize the right of one injured by a drunken driver to sue the person who had served the drunk the drinks.[6] The Pennsylvania court refused to disturb the Pennsylvania legislature's plan for local funding of the state's public schools.[7] The Idaho court refused to follow the lead of progressive state courts and allow a suit against a person who negligently caused emotional injury unless the negligence had also caused physical injury.[8] These courts chose not to be significant policy makers for their states.

The policy making by the Indiana, West Virginia, and Ohio courts was obviously of general importance in these states. The importance of this power of state supreme courts to make policy has been magnified by two changes that occurred at the national level during the 1980s and 1990s. The U.S. Supreme Court assured state courts that it would not review their decisions that are clearly based in the state's own constitution,[9] which effectively makes these courts totally autonomous in their decisions that change policy as long as they follow the U.S. Supreme Court's direction. The state court can now be the final authority in state policy issues. This judicial policy autonomy is joined by the increased policy discretion that state legislators and state administrators have been given by the devolution of responsibility and policy control as a result of the increased use of block grants that have characterized recent sessions of Congress.

The convergence of the potential autonomy that state courts enjoy and increased state policy discretion has made the state court, potentially, a very important policy maker in an increasingly important policy arena. There has been relatively little study of policy making by state courts. What has been done has been directed toward better understanding of the *policy produced* rather than to the basic decision whether or not to produce it. There has been no investigation of what causes some state courts to embrace the policy-making role and others to reject it.

POLICY MAKING

Policy making is what governments choose to do or not to do—specifically the regulation of behavior and the distribution of benefits.[10] Courts routinely establish policy by their decisions, even in their most mundane cases. Every court necessarily makes policy each time it decides a case: it distributes burdens and benefits between or among the parties. Even when courts only decide disputes between the parties to a case, the establishment of limited policy is important to the maintenance of social order. However, this policy making is necessarily limited to a regulation of, or distribution of benefits between or among, the selfishly interested parties to the case. The judicial policy decisions that allowed a victim of a drunk bar customer to sue the bar, that required the state to support public education equally throughout the state, and that forced insurance companies to compensate victims of intrafamily accidents had effects far beyond the parties to the cases because they changed the established policy of their states.

Definition of Intentional Activism

Only when a court makes policy that regulates behavior or distributes benefits according to its collective preferences (or those of its majority) and different from the regulation or distribution prescribed by another authoritative policy maker is it the equal to its state's legislature and governor. Judicial modification of established policy is the result of a court's being active, being an "activist" court. A "court is activist when its decisions conflict with those of other political policy makers."[11] This definition of judicial activism is both succinct and "precise"[12] and it serves a subsidiary and related interest in establishing the relative importance of state supreme courts and state legislatures and governors as policy makers. It will guide this work with the clarifying enlargement: "A court is activist when its decisions conflict with those of other political policy makers, *including predecessor courts*."[13] An activist court has implicitly considered established policy and has either struck it down or reversed it as a necessary preliminary to the establishment of its preferred policy. Intentional, active judicial policy making occurs only when a court effectively disagrees with a legislature, a predecessor court, or initiates a new policy. It effectively disagrees with a legislature when it invalidates a law that the legislature has passed; it effectively disagrees with an earlier court when it overrules policy that has become judicial doctrine, such as parental immunity; and it intentionally and actively initiates official policy when its decision recognizes a cause of action that hadn't previously existed. Such intentional, active judicial policy making establishes a state supreme court on the same policy-making level as its state's governor and legislature.[14]

U.S. Supreme Court Activism. Most study of judicial activism has been focused on the U.S. Supreme Court. Interest in the Court's activism was engendered by the prominence of the Court's policy-making economic decisions during the 1930s and its civil rights/civil liberties policy-making decisions during the 1950s and 1960s. This prominence raised normative questions of the proper role of the Court,[15] which was the principle interest of the attention to the Court's activism. There was no interest in explaining the determinants of the Court's decision to make policy; all seemed to be satisfied with the underlying assumption that ideological differences between the members of the Court's majorities and the Congress and president or the states' policy makers was the cause. This focus on the Supreme Court made any investigation of the impetus for policy making difficult because there was no comparison of its action with other action. Perhaps this difficulty, coupled with satisfaction with the assumption that ideological differences were the cause, made further study seem of little value. For whatever reason, the great preponderance of attention to judicial activism and policy making was devoted to description rather than explanation.[16]

From its beginning, the Supreme Court has been an important national policy maker. The first Supreme Court, in 1793, in one of its first decisions, abrogated the established common law doctrine of states' immunity from suit, sovereign immunity. Justice James Wilson, of that Court, recognized that the issue before the Court in that case was one of "uncommon magnitude" and framed the issue in the case in terms of national policy: would not state sovereign immunity "be repugnant to our very existence as a nation?"[17] The power of judicial review that has enabled American courts to declare legislative acts invalid rests in part on Chief Justice John Marshall's consideration, in a later case, of the effect of a policy that would not recognize the Constitution as superior to an ordinary legislative act: such a "doctrine would subvert the very foundation of all written constitutions . . . (and) would declare that if a legislature should do what is expressly forbidden, such act . . . is in reality effectual."[18] Later, Chief Justice Marshall took the Court into the simmering policy controversy over the relative powers of the national and state governments and concluded that: "the interests of the nation" and its "happiness and prosperity" depended on the full execution by the national government of the powers enumerated in Article I, Section 8 of the Constitution.[19]

When the validity of the institution of slavery became the consuming issue in national life, the Court entered the controversy with its controversial but consequential decision in the *Dred Scott* case,[20] in which Chief Justice Taney considered that the policy of the Missouri Compromise "deprives a citizen of his property . . . merely because he brought (it) into a particular territory of the United States," a policy effect that Taney concluded could not be "dignified with the name of due process." During the turbulent period of the Great Depression the Court was at the center of national policy making. During the first four years of Franklin Roosevelt's New Deal the court regularly reversed the policy of the Roosevelt Administration and Congress: if the congressional policy would be allowed to prevail, "there would be virtually no limit to the federal power and for all practical purpose we should have a completely centralized government."[21] After the celebrated "shift" of 1937 following Roosevelt's landslide 1936 reelection, it was the Court that announced that the national government had practically unlimited power to regulate the national economy.[22]

U.S. Supreme Court Justices—Experienced Policy Makers. These Supreme Court decisions exemplify important judicial policy making. There is a significant differences between the levels of policy making in the U.S. Supreme Court and the various state courts, as well as differences in the government experience of the respective justices prior to their joining their courts. The range of the levels of policy making between and among state courts is wide, while the Supreme Court has participated in making national policy throughout American history. Judicial policy making on the Supreme Court came naturally to justices who had routinely made important policy decisions in their pre-Court official positions. Service in a high position in government is the "last step" on the path to the U.S. Supreme Court.[23] One hundred and eleven justices have served or are serving on the Supreme Court and a substantial number of these had experience in a policy-making governmental office prior to their ascension to the Court. Sixty-five had previously served in the executive branch of the federal government. Thirty-five had served in the U.S. Congress. Fifty-two future Supreme Court justices served in state legislatures and forty-five had held positions in a state's executive branch.[24] In contrast with the justice's prior policy-making experience in the executive and legislative branches of government, only thirteen of the one hundred and eleven ascended the Supreme Court bench with only judicial experience.[25] The predominance of policy-making experience over exclusively judicial experience of the Supreme Court's justices is an important difference between the Court and the fifty state courts.

It is notable that each of the five justices who wrote the Supreme Court's opinions in the five landmark policy-making cases previously described, had substantial policy-making experience in the legislative and executive branches of the state and national governments but only one had any prior judicial experience.[26] The exception, John Marshall, had served one two-year term as a member of the Richmond, Virginia, Hustings court, but, significantly, his policy-making experience eclipsed this judicial experience in both extent and importance: Member, Virginia House of Delegates; Member, Virginia Governor's Council of State; Delegate, Virginia Constitutional Ratifying Convention; Member, U.S. Diplomatic Mission to France; Member, U.S. House of Representatives; U.S. Secretary of State.[27] The service of the other four similarly reached to the highest level of national policy making: Justice Wilson (*Chisholm v. Georgia*), Member, Philadelphia Constitutional Convention; Chief Justice Taney (*Dred Scott v. Sandford*), U.S. Secretary of the Treasury; Chief Justice Hughes (*Schecter Poultry Corp. v. United States*), U.S. Secretary of State; and Chief Justice Stone (*United States v. Darby*), U.S. Attorney General.[28]

TWO-PART PROCESS

The First Part

The process of individual decision-making that ultimately results in new judicially made policy, at least by state courts, is a two-part decision-making process by the individual judge.[29] For the first part, the judge must decide whether it is proper for a judge to act in the circumstance of a pending case in a way that will produce a new or changed policy—that is, whether the judge thinks that policy making is proper judicial behavior in the pending case. The judge must answer the question: does my perception of my role as judge allow me to use my position to impose my personal preference to create new policy or upset established policy on these facts?

The decision that the judge makes in the first part of the process is crucial. If the judge answers "no," that the judge's perceived judicial role denies him/her the freedom to act consistently with his/her preferences in the instant case, that is the end of any possible participation by the judge in a judicial change in policy. The judge will not participate in intentional judicial policy making by the court. Only if the judge decides, in the first part of the process, that policy making is proper judicial behavior will the judge be free to allow his/her attitude, or preference to contribute to intentional judicial policy making.

Justice Richard Neely of the West Virginia court, explained his dissent from his court's important policy-making decision that West Virginia's legislatively prescribed policy for paying for public schools violated the West Virginia Constitution:[30]

> I finally concluded that the political role of the courts is . . . not determining how much money and people should be thrown at what; thus I dissented from the majority opinion. It is, nevertheless, difficult to criticize a majority which is trying to make life better for the most deprived children in their jurisdiction.[31]

Although his preference was for the school finance policy established by his court's majority, his preferred judicial role, restrained in the area of public finance, precluded him from joining the majority's policy-making decision.

In another area of judicial activity, that of sentencing convicted defendants by trial judges, the judge's role[32] orientation has been demonstrated to control whether the judge's personal preferences will affect the severity of the sentence imposed on convicted criminal defendants.[33] The sentencing decision by trial court judges is judicial policy making at the trial court level.[34] In this judicial decision making, role orientation intervenes between the sentencing judge's attitude and the judge's behavior, the sentence, and specifies the criteria on which the sentencing decisions can be made.[35] Role orientation will determine the legitimacy of allowing criteria test have no strictly legal base to influence decision making, sentencing.[36]

Justice Neely in the school finance case and a sentencing trial court judge each engaged in a judicial policy-making process and each had to first decide whether their preferred judicial role allowed them to consult their personal preferences in making their decisions. Justice Neely decided the first part question negatively, that his understanding was that it was not the proper role for a state court judge to determine fiscal policy in public education and, consequently, his personal policy preference became immaterial. Similarly, a sentencing trial judge must first decide whether his/her personal preference may properly influence the sentence decision, and only if the answer is affirmative, will the judge consider personal, nonlegal influences, his/her attitude in passing sentence. Before judges allow personal policy preferences to influence their judicial decisions they must decide whether their judicial role conception permits such influence. A judge who is restrained by a narrow role orientation may not legitimately allow his or her own preferences to influence decision making while, on the other hand, judges who view their personal attitudes as having a legitimate role in decision making may allow their personal preferences to influence their decision making.

This first part of the process is basic. We can conjecture that a likely influence on this decision is the judge's socialization in the law. Secondary and collegiate education routinely teach the future judge that the legislature is the proper governmental policy-making institution. When the future judge attends an American law school he or she is indoctrinated with the idea of the stability of the decided case and its importance in deciding similar subsequent cases. This is because American law schools rely almost exclusively on appellate judicial opinions as texts for the study of "the law" and emphasize the importance of precedent to courts when they decide cases, the "case method." This combination of belief in the propriety of legislative policy making and in the stability of the decided case and reliance on it as the source of "the law" would preclude a decision to reverse the legislature or overrule doctrine that has been established by an earlier court. If this effect of a judge's education is not overcome, the judge will view a restrained judicial role as proper.[37] The likely stability of this role decision and its remoteness from the immediate judicial decision obscures it, giving the impression that judicial decision making has only one stage. Because this decision has probably been made on the basis of influences that operate prior to a judge's ascension to the bench, it will not be reviewed at the time that each decision the judge makes occurs but will continue to control the judge until it is disturbed. The influence of a fellow judge who is an advocate of intentional judicial activism is one extraordinary stimulus in the judicial decision-making process that can disturb a judge's settled role decision.

The Second Part

The second part of the judge's decision is whether the judge prefers a new policy or one that is different from that inherent in the legislative act or the established judicial doctrine. This choice is only faced by judges who have previously decided that their role perception permit them to allow their policy preferences to create new policy or to impact established legislative or judicial policy. The judges who are restrained by their role decision will participate in policy making only within the context of the case and only as it affects the case participants. Judges who are not restrained by their role decision may participate in making intentional policy. If an emancipated judge prefers the established policy he/she will affirm the legislative act or established doctrine. In such case, the judge's policy making will be invisible and indistinguishable from that of the earlier judicial or legislative policy maker. However, if the judge's policy choice is different from that of the prior policy maker and is ultimately expressed in the court's decision, he/she will have participated in intentional judicial policy making. When a state court changes established policy, it becomes the policy making equal of its state's governor and legislature.[38]

There can be many relationships between a judge's judicial role conception and the judge's attitudes or preferences. Research based on sentences for guilty defendants illuminates the relation between the judicial role of proper sentencing behavior and the judge's attitude; Neely's dissent illuminates the relation between a judge's role and the judge's preferred policy when considering the constitutionality of a legislatively mandated state policy. Other possible relationships are those between a judge's role and the judge's preferred policy when considering the policy contained in administrative rules and regulations;[39] in considering a of doctrine-laden precedent; and when the judge is considering the initial promulgation of governmental policy.[40] Each of these describes a relationship that is similar to those of the sentencing judge and to Justice Neely in his dissent in the West Virginia court's school finance case. We can assume that a judge's role threshold for initial establishment of policy would be different from the role threshold for overruling common-law doctrine or for declaring an administrative rule or regulation or a legislative act unconstitutional. Our interest is limited to the relationships between state supreme court justices' roles in (a) declaring state law unconstitutional, (b) reversing doctrine-laden precedent, and (c) promulgating new governmental policy. In other words, the relationship between roles and policy preferences of justices who are members of courts that make intentional, active policy.

Difference between State Courts and the Supreme Court

Supreme Court justices may not make their decisions in two parts; they may not first consider the question whether it is proper for judges to make policy. In other words, there may not have been a restrained justice on the Supreme Court, at least recently.[41] With Supreme Court justices the initial decision of the two-part process may have been stabilized by their substantial pre-Court exercise of policy making at a high level. Any initial choice of a restrained role in policy making may have been overcome by experience in regularly making policy in their high government jobs. Apparently, Supreme Court justices' attitudes and personal preferences, constrain most if not all, their decision making.[42] However, the state courts are, in this respect, different from the Supreme Court. Different pre-high court experiences, normative expectations, limited tenures, and levels of docket control of the respective courts make the state court judges' judicial policy-making process substantially different from that of their Supreme Court counterparts.

The predominant pre-Court governmental experience of Supreme Court justices has been in high level positions in the executive branch of the federal government, a significant number had also served in Congress.[43] In contrast with the justice's prior policy-making experience in executive and legislative positions, a small minority had joined the Supreme Court with only judicial experience.[44] Unlike their Supreme Court brethren, state court judges' predominant governmental experience has been on inferior state courts or attenuated service in state legislatures. Unlike the prior experience of the Supreme Court justices, the pre-high court governmental experience of most of the justices of the activist 1980s courts that we will examine was either nonexistent or limited to service on lower state courts. Fifty-eight percent of these state court judges had served only on inferior state court benches or had no prior governmental experience.[45] Policy making requires considerations of the goals toward which policy is directed and the effects that it will have. Because courts are structured hierarchically, judicial experience on an inferior state court gives a judge a very limited opportunity to make policy. Considerations of goals and effects are not components of judicial decision making by inferior state courts; cases are decided as required by constitutions, statutes, precedent, and logic regardless of the court's goals or the decision's effect. Experience as an inferior state court judge reinforces the non-activist preference that is engendered by American legal education.

The normative expectation that judges should not intrude into the legislative domain of policy making resonates more powerfully in the states than it does in Washington, especially in the selection of the respective courts' judges. The necessity that state court justices campaign to win electoral, gubernatorial, or legislative approval in order to get and keep their jobs makes the expectation that judges should not usurp the policy-making legislative role imperative in the state courts but not with Supreme Court justices with their life tenure. State judges who are in danger of being charged with overstepping their authority when their jobs are on the line are more likely to be deferential in their approach to policy making. One prominent state court judge who ignored the expected deference suffered negative electoral consequences. In the 1986 Ohio chief justice election in which Chief Justice Frank Celebrezze was trying to keep his job, the question of his failure to defer to the legislature was raised by opposition forces. The public issue of the campaign that defeated him was the charge that his judicial behavior was "improper."[46] In Washington, the effect of deference may be opposite of the effect that it has in the states. The expectations of the president, the singularly most important person in the selection of Supreme Court justices, is the opposite of the norm of deference: presidents do not want the justices that they nominate to be deferential; they reasonably expect and want the justices they nominate *to* engage in policy making on the Court, at least with respect to the appointing president's preferred policy. Presumably, a president will appoint a justice whom he or she thinks is "attitudinally" compatible and the president will, naturally, want that justice to express their shared attitude in Supreme Court decision making. The more diffuse and fleeting relationship between candidates for seats on state court benches and their "selectors," particularly in states that elect their justices,[47] makes this desire by the selector unreasonable and unlikely.

Other differences between the circumstances of state courts and the Supreme

Court that militate for judicial restraint in the states are the lifetime tenure of Supreme Court justices that frees them of any restraint on their expression of their attitudes that might be caused by concern over their re-selection, a freedom that state court judges have in only three states.[48] The almost absolute control that the Supreme Court has over which appeals it will hear and decide allows the justices to limit their time and consideration to cases that pique their attitudes. With the exception of the West Virginia court,[49] state constitutions and statutes require state court judges to hear and decide appeals in cases in areas of the law in which the justices' attitudes are often not engaged. Possible legislative budget retaliation and gubernatorial refusal to enforce the courts' decisions are other considerations that might explain restrained judicial decision-making on state courts,[50] although neither is very likely nor much different from similar federal expectation.[51] One activist advocate whom we will examine closely, the Honorable Randall Shepard of the Indiana Supreme Court, clearly believes that state court policy making has two parts. He concluded that these judges use their own state constitution's provisions rather than the federal constitutional because they aspire to be "independent sources of the law" rather than because they "desire to continue . . . the agenda of the Warren-Brennan Court."[52]

THE ACTIVIST ADVOCATE

Minority Influence

The "judicial role" model is considerably more influential than the "attitudinal" model in state courts. A state court that has at least one judge who advocates an active judicial role for any reason is more likely to intentionally and actively make policy than a court without such an advocate.[53] The presence of this activist advocate on a court can be a stimulus that causes other members of the court to reconsider their established role decisions. The introduction to a court of a judge who believes that activism and policy making are proper judicial roles and who advocates active decision making can change a non-activist, non-policy-making court into an active court that intentionally participates in making policy for its state. This phenomenon of human behavior has been recognized in psychology as "minority influence."[54] Psychologists have recognized that groups strive for agreement and have concluded that when a minority of the group introduces new, unexpected information that causes the group to examine group issues more carefully, that examination may result in acceptance of the minority view. The pressure on the *majority* to change becomes "explosive" when the advocating minority cannot be excluded from the group, as no member of a court can be legitimately excluded from a court's decision making.[55]

Minority influence has been felt in American appellate courts. In the early 1940s, the Supreme Court changed from an appellate court in which there were very few dissenting or concurring opinions to a court in which a substantial majority of its opinions[56] were issued with dissents or concurrences as a result of Chief Justice Harlan Stone's advocacy of dissent as an important aid in the development of "sound legal principles."[57] The advocacy of dissent as a legitimate part of the judicial decision-making process by only one justice out of nine caused the Supreme Court to reconsider its norm of consensus and changed that Court's norm from consensus to dissensus.[58]

On a more mundane level, we are familiar with a group in a formal situation, perhaps in a church, that is soberly restrained from laughing at something obviously funny until the first person snickers, which breaks the ice and can leave the group in stitches. The judge who introduces the idea of judicial activism and policy making to a restrained state court causes the other judges to look more carefully at their ideas of judicial propriety just as Chief Justice Stone caused the Supreme Court to reconsider its norm of consensus. This closer examination can lead the restrained majority that is striving for agreement to conclude that judicial activism and policy making can be proper behavior for a state supreme court. Such agreement may result in a paroxysm of judicial policy making. Recently, a spasm of policy making erupted in the Indiana, West Virginia, and Ohio courts following the introduction to these courts of a committed activist advocate. The contrast between the policy explosions by these three courts after they were joined by the activist advocate with the paucity of policy decisions by courts without such advocate will show the probable importance of such advocates in the decision by a court to become a policy maker. Compare Chapters 2, 3, and 4 with Chapter 5.

State courts have historically provided a link between the current democracy of state legislatures and the fundamental authority of the U.S. Constitution. Until the 1980s, the importance of these state courts was diminished by the threat that the Supreme Court would upset their most important policy decisions on appeal. However, the Supreme Court has clarified the states' courts preeminent role in interpreting their own constitutions. Since the 1930s and until recently, Congress had effectively preempted much of the policy-making field previously occupied by state legislatures leaving the states a very limited range of independent policy action. Congress has begun to return increasing authority and responsibility to the states. The outcome of these developments has created a potential for state courts to become the final arbiter in a greatly increased array of basic policy issues. These developments have immeasurably augmented the policy-making importance of these courts. This increased potential importance of state courts demands an understanding of the difference between courts that participate as intentional active policy makers in their states and those that do not.

The presence of just one judge who is an advocate of intentional, active policy making increases the likelihood that a state court will intentionally make policy in its state. To fully explain this conclusion, this chapter has described the two-part process that individual state court judges must complete before they will participate in judicial policy making, particularly the first part of the process in which the activist advocate can be influential. An explanation of the significance of a single judge is found in the psychological phenomenon of "minority influence," in which the minority in a small group has the power to cause the majority to consider the minority's views and adopt them. Current description of this phenomenon has been summarized to demonstrate its application to the process that courts undergo in making the basic first decision that policy making is an acceptable judicial role. The participation of the Supreme Court in policy making throughout its history and the policy-making backgrounds of its justices were illuminated to compare its similarities to state courts that participate in their states' policy making and to contrast its differences with those state courts that refrain from making policy.

The remainder of this book will support more fully the conclusion that one justice who advocates judicial activism makes it more likely that his/her court will become a policy maker. Chapters 2, 3, and 4 will separately describe policy making in the three state courts of Indiana, West Virginia, and Ohio during recent similar periods for the purpose of establishing these courts as intentional policy makers. We will examine the recent history of each court, survey the backgrounds of the justices of these courts in order to uncover their judicial philosophy, and closely scrutinize the biographies of three justice, one from each court, who have been identified as intentional activist advocates. We will also undertake a case-by-case survey of the decisions that each court made in cases in which the court could have made policy.

The decisions and personnel of the supreme courts of the neighboring states of Indiana, West Virginia, and Ohio during the 1970s and 1980s are ideal for a study of intentional, activist judicial policy making. Judicial policy making came alive during this period in each of these state courts and each court had reached the nadir of activism during the preceding decade. This preference for the active judicial role is the only temporal coincidence among them. Activism did not begin at the same time nor did it exist simultaneously in the three courts. Nor has activism apparently achieved the same permanence in the three states. It seems to be firmly planted in Indiana; assured of continued, though uneven, flower in West Virginia, and may have begun to fade in Ohio.

The national reputations of the courts in these states have spanned the range during their histories. The Indiana Supreme Court had been among the leading state courts in the nation but had slid to mediocrity by 1980; West Virginia's Supreme Court was, by some measures, near the bottom of the pecking order, historically and in 1976; and the Ohio Supreme Court was plugging along determinedly in mediocrity until the judicial election of 1978. Over much of the judicial history of the states, the Indiana court could have made a strong claim to one of the top rungs of the states' judicial quality ladder. During West Virginia's attenuated history, its court has done its business with little claim to notice. Although Ohio had been able to claim leadership among the states in some contributions to the nation's government, it can claim only a firm grasp on the middle ground of the states' courts.[59]

West Virginia, Ohio, and Indiana form a band of states across the eastern midsection of the United States from the Blue Ridge Mountains of Virginia in the east to the prairies of Illinois in the west. Although these states are contiguous, their geography, history, economy, and politics are distinct. West Virginia can claim a share, with Virginia, of the motherhood of many of our earlier presidents and it was born of the strains and wounds of the Civil War. Ohio's claim to the presidency is to later and less distinguished incumbents and its birth was earlier and much more joyful than West Virginia's, bearing the promise of the Northwest Ordinance. Indiana's birth could pass unremarked except for the inconvenience of frontier Indian skirmishes, and its subsequent experiences have been unremarkable.

The business activities and produce of the three are varied: West Virginia produces coal in its southern mountains and steel in its northern panhandle and, as a result of the basic nature of its economy, it has suffered wild economic fluctuations. The Ohio economy is more varied, and consequently somewhat more stable, with basic manufacturing in the northeast and smaller and more diversified manufacturing and agriculture across its central hills and plains and its southern counties. Indiana also has a relatively stable, predominantly agricultural and service economy and experiences only localized economic dislocation, mirroring the fortunes of the predominant basic industry in its northwest corner. The successes of the major political parties in controlling each of these states' governors' offices and legislatures has been mixed, Republicans have been predominant in the control of both the governor's office and the legislature in Indiana; Democrats and Republicans have alternated in the control of the governor's office and the Democrats have usually controlled the statehouse in West Virginia; and the parties have taken their turns in Ohio. Consistently, Republican justices have predominated on the Indiana Supreme Court, Democrats on the West Virginia Supreme Court of Appeals, and the parties have successively shared the majority on recent Ohio courts, with the Republicans having the historical edge.

Chapter 2 will describe Indiana judicial activism; Chapter 3 will depict activist decision making in the West Virginia court, and Chapter 4 will illuminate judicial policy making in the Ohio court.

Chapter 5 will describe judicial role preferences and decision making in the courts of three states—Idaho, Florida, and Pennsylvania—whose judges did not exhibit a preference for the judicial activist role, for periods comparable to those of Chapters 2, 3, and 4, with attention to the opportunities these courts had to make policy by their decisions.

In Chapter 6, the contrast between the decision making and the judicial philosophies of the judges described in Chapters 2, 3, and 4 and those in Chapter 5 will illuminate the conclusion that an activist advocate makes it more likely that a state court will be an intentional, activist policy maker in its state. A comparison of three policy-making courts will eliminate other characteristics of state supreme courts as necessary or sufficient causes of active judicial policy making. These comparisons will also suggest that the motives that impel the activists' advocacy may determine the stability of resulting judicial policy making by the court.

NOTES

1. *Piccadilly, Inc. v. Colvey* (1980) 519 N.E. 2d 1217.

2. *Pauley v. Kelly*, 255 S.E. 2d 859 (1979).

3. *Kirchner v. Chrystal*, 474 N.E. 2d 275 (1984).

4. *Shearer v. Shearer*, 480 N.E. 2d 388 (1985).

5. Hereinafter, I will refer to the highest appellate state courts as the "Indiana court," the "West Virginia court" and the "Ohio court" or as "the court," as the context indicates; to the U.S. Supreme Court as "the Supreme Court" or as "the Court," as the context indicates; and to courts, generally, as "courts."

6. *Bankston, et ux. v. Brennen, et al.*, 507 So.2d 1385 (1987).

7. *Danson, et ux. etc. v. Casey et al.*, 399 A.2d 360 (1979).

8. *Hathaway v. Krumery*, 716 P.2d 1287 (1986).

9. *Michigan v. Long*, 463 U.S. 1032 (1983).

10. Thomas R. Dye, *Understanding Public Policy* (Englewood Cliffs, N.J.: Prentice-Hall, 1992).

11. Bradley C. Canon, "A Framework for the Analysis of Judicial Activism," in *Supreme Court Activism and Restraint*, Stephen C. Halpern and Charles M. Lamb, eds. (Lexington, Mass.: Lexington Books, 1982), pp. 385–419. Canon quoted Glendon Schubert's definition as found in David Forte's *The Supreme Court: Judicial Activism Versus Judicial Restraint* (Lexington, Mass.: D. C. Heath, 1972).

12. Canon, "A Framework," p. 385

13. A court also intentionally makes policy when it initiates a political policy in an area in which there is no existing policy. In the terms of Schubert's definition, such circumstance is the court's disagreement with other policy makers that there should not have been policy in such area.

14. There are many different dimensions of judicial activism. I am interested in this particular dimension because it helps locate state courts in the state policy-making hierarchy. Bradley Canon surveys and describes other dimensions in "A Framework."

15. For three different perspectives on the normative question, see Louis A. Gaglia, "In Defense of Judicial Restraint," Arthur S. Miller, "In Defense of Judicial Activism," and Henry J Abraham, "Line Drawing Between Judicial Activism and Judicial Restraint: A 'Centrist' Approach and Analysis," all in *Supreme Court Activism and Restraint*, Stephen C. Halpern and Charles M. Lamb, eds.

16. Bradley Canon has summarized the important literature on activism in the Supreme Court in "A Framework."

17. *Chisolm v. Georgia*, 2 Dall (2U.S.) 419 (1793).

18. *Marbury v. Madison*, 1 Cranch (5 U.S.) 137 (1803).

19. *McCulloch v. Maryland*, 4 Wheaton (17 U.S.) 316 (1819).

20. *Dred Scott v. Sandford*, 60 U.S. (19 Howard) 393 (1857).

21. *Schecter Poultry Corp. v. United States*, 295 U.S. 495 (1935).

22. *United States v. Darby*, 312 U.S. 100 (1941).

23. Lawrence Baum, *The Supreme Court*, fifth ed. (Washington, D.C.: CQ Press, 1995).

24. Craig R. Ducat, *Constitutional Interpretation* (Minneapolis: West Publishing, 1996).

25. One of the thirteen, Justice Horace Lurton, served on both state and lower federal benches prior to serving on the Supreme Court. Of the remaining twelve justices whose only prior government service was judicial, eight had served only on state courts and four had served only on lower federal courts.

26. Ducat, *Constitutional Interpretation*, pp. A6–A14.

27. Clare Cushman, ed., *The Supreme Court Justices* (Washington: CQ Press, 1995), pp. 61–65.

28. Ducat, *Constitutional Interpretation*, pp. A6–A14.

29. Attention will be predominantly to the states' highest courts, whose members universally have the title of "justice." However, members of state Courts will be referred to, herein, as "judges."

30. *Pauley v. Kelly*, 255 S.E.2d 859 (1979).

31. The Hon. Richard Neely, *How Courts Govern America* (New Haven, Conn.: Yale University Press, 1981) p. 173. Neely voted *with the majority* on the first vote on this decision in conference, an indication that his policy preference, attitude, opposed the existing policy. See Neely, *How Courts*, p. 186.

32. Role, or judicial role, is an ambiguous term that can have many meanings. I use the term to refer only to judicial policy making: an intentionally activist judicial role allows a judge to participate in policy making by initiating official policy by recognizing a cause of action that had not previously existed, change policy by overruling an earlier decision that had established a definitive common law rule, and change or alter legislative policy by invalidating a law passed by the legislature. A restrained role precludes such participation.

33. James L. Gibson, "Judges Role Orientations, Attitudes and Decisions: An Interactive Model," *The American Political Science Review* 72 (1978): 911–924.

34. George W. Pruitt and Henry R. Glick, "Social Environment, Public Opinion, and Judicial Policymaking," *American Politics Quarterly*, 14 (Nos. 1 and 2, 1986): 5–33.

35. Gibson, "Judges Role," p. 922.

36. Gibson, "Judges Role," p. 922. Gibson's groundbreaking study was a search for an explanation of the independent contributions that judge's role orientations and judge's attitudes make to judicial decision making. Earlier research had indicated that judicial orientation, a judge's belief about the propriety of certain judicial behavior, and a judge's attitude, the judge's preferences, are each

important predictors of the judge's decision, but no one had explained how these characteristics acted together on the decision making. Gibson studied the behavior of trial court judges in sentencing convicted criminals; the role choice between the propriety of using only "legal criteria" and using "criteria that have no strictly legal base" to decide the sentence; and the judicial preference was the judge's level of "liberalism."

37. The effect of the future judge's law school education is less likely to be "restraining" if the law school is a national rather than local law school. An education at a national law school could lead the judge to an activist role. National law schools, because their graduates are likely to be dispersed among a number of states, include within their curricula the various approaches to any given problem that are taken throughout the country, including the most innovative, while local law schools concentrate on the state of the law within their locale, that which their graduates are likely to encounter in their practices. A judge with a broad legal education will know of the range of available and generally acceptable solutions to the problem and will be more likely to try a new solution. A national law school education is a likely stimulus that could overcome any lingering restraining effect of the judge's earlier education. Local law schools are, typically, the law schools of the state universities and national law schools are typically private law schools with substantial reputations, such as the law schools of Harvard, Columbia, Duke, Harvard, Northwestern, Stanford, and Yale Universities and the Universities of Chicago, Michigan, and Pennsylvania. This listing is illustrative and not exhaustive.

38. There is a limitation on even the most active state court that the governor and the legislature do not have. The court must wait until an issue is brought to it for decision, unlike the governor or legislature that can initiate policy making. However, a court's reputation for activism might encourage a party who wants a statute reversed, precedent overruled, or new doctrine established to bring an appropriate case to the court.

39. There is a judicial rule for interpretation of administrative action that assumes that an administrative rule, regulation, or decision that has been made by an administrative agency and that survives one session of the legislature without legislative change has received the tacit approval of that legislature.

40. A similar opportunity for judicial policy making occurs when a court interprets a vague or generally phrased legislation regulation. This type of judicial policy making is excluded from this study because of the difficulty (if not impossibility) of concluding that there has been a judicial change in the legislatively established policy.

41. Jeffrey A. Segal and Harold J. Spaeth, *The Supreme Court and the Attitudinal Model* (New York: Cambridge University Press, 1993).

42. Or, perhaps, Supreme Court policy making has been so pervasive that it has become institutionalized and the institution obviates the first step.

43. Ducat, *Constitutional Interpretation*, pp. A6–A14.

44. Ducat, *Constitutional Interpretation*, pp. A6–A14.

45. Those state court justices whose only prior governmental experience had been on inferior state court benches were: De Bruler, Prentice, Pivarnik, Hunter and Dickson (Indiana); McGraw, Miller and Harshbarger (West Virginia); C. Brown, H. Brown, Krupansky, J. Celebrezze, Wright, Sweeney, and Resnick (Ohio).

46. Lawrence Baum, "State Supreme Courts: Activism and Accountability," in the *State of the States*, Carl E. Van Horn, ed. (Washington, D.C.: CQ Press, 1982), p. 125. In that same election, Craig Wright, a candidate for associate justice who was to be successful, "aired some tough television ads complaining of the court's attempt to "legislate."" "Politics Defeats Two Democrat Justices," *The Los Angeles Daily Journal* 97 (Nov, 8, 1988): 5. After that election, the successful candidate for chief justice, Thomas R. Moyer, announced that he understood "that judges are not legislators in robes." The Hon. Thomas R. Moyer, "The Supreme Court of Ohio: Restoration of an Institution," *Ohio State Bar Association Report* 60 (Jan. 6, 1987): 84.

47. Election is the method used by the largest number of state, twenty-three. *Book of the States*, Vol. 31 (Lexington, Ky.: The Council of State Governments, 1996), pp. 133–35.

48. The justices of the Massachusetts and New Hampshire courts may serve "until age seventy" and the Rhode Island justices serve "for life." *Book of the States*, Vol. 31 (Lexington, Ky.: The Council of State Governments, 1996), pp. 127–8.

49. See West Virginia Constitution, Article 8, Section 4.

50. Justice Neely of the West Virginia court has suggested an interesting difference between the Supreme Court and state courts: that the "parochialism" of state courts might cause these courts to be restrained when considering state policy that may be "unfair" to out-of-state interests, a parochialism that the Supreme Court would not share. The Hon. Richard Neely, *How Courts Govern America* (New Haven, Conn.: Yale University Press, 1981), p. 99.

51. Studies of state court decision making have demonstrated that influences other than a judge's attitude may influence the state judge's decision. An interesting examination of the incidence of dissent in the Rhode Island court concludes that there was a norm in that court that the justices should agree formally in the court's opinions regardless of serious disagreement with the opinion's conclusion. During three years in which that court collectively made 2,225 individual decisions, only 1 1/3 percent of these decisions were in disagreement with the court's opinion: thirteen dissenting and two concurring. The norm and not the judge's attitude apparently determined the judge's decision. Edward N. Beiser, "The Rhode Island Supreme Court: A Well Integrated Political System," *Law and Society* 8 (1974):167–186. Another examination of the decision by state court

judges to dissent found that institutional characteristics of the court system had significant effects on that decision. Melinda Gann Hall and Paul Brace, "Order in the Courts: A Neo-Institutional Approach to Judicial Consensus," *Western Political Quarterly* 42 (1989): 391.

52. The Hon. Randall J. Shepard, "The Maturing Nature of State Constitution Jurisprudence," *Valparaiso University Law Review* 30, (Spring 1996): 421–57, 421.

53. Charles S. Lopeman, "Activism in State Supreme Courts," Ph.D. diss. The Ohio State University, 1995.

54. Serge Muscovici, "Social Influence and Conformity*,*" *Handbook of Social Psychology*, Gardner Lindsey and Elliot Aronson, eds. (New York: Random House, 1985), pp. 347–412; Elliot Aronson, Timothy D. Wilson, and Robin Akert, *Social Psychology*, second ed. (New York: Longman Press, 1997).

55. Muscovici, "Social Influence," p. 356.

56. "Prior to 1941 an average of 8.5 dissenting opinions were issued for every 100 majority opinions, but after 1941 that figure rose to seventy-three dissenting opinions." Thomas G. Walker, Lee Epstein, and William Dixon, "On the Mysterious Demise of Consensual Norms in the United States Supreme Court," *The Journal of Politics* 50 (1988): 361, 362.

57. Walker, et al., "On the Mysterious," p. 379.

58. That Stone was the chief justice is likely not significant in his influence in changing this norm. Chief Justice Rehnquist believes that the chiefs' influence results from skill at persuading or cajoling the associate brethren rather than from the power of the position. He has described the eight associates as "independent as hogs on ice." Lawrence Baum, *The Supreme Court*, fifth ed. (Washington, D.C.: CQ Press, 1995), p. 178. The formal powers of the chief justiceship, to preside over oral argument and conferences, to establish the initial listing of cases for the court's docket, and to assign opinion writing (Baum, *The Supreme Court*, p. 178.) would seem to be irrelevant to influencing the individual associate justices to adopt the norm of dissensus.

59. Gregory Caldeira, "On the reputation of State Courts," *Political Behavior* 5 (1983): 83; Bradley C. Canon and Lawrence Baum, "Patterns of Adoption of Tort Law Innovation: An Application of Diffusion Theory to Judicial Doctrines," *American Political Science Review* 75 (19981): 975–987; Rodney L. Mott, "Judicial Influence," *American Political Science Review* 30 (1936): 295–315.

Chapter 2

Indiana

Indiana is the center of the Midwest's three-state eastern panhandle. Its northwest industrial corridor, from Gary to South Bend, is "really an extension of the Chicago metropolitan area"[1] and its straight-line western and eastern boundaries make no distinction from neighboring Illinois and Ohio farmland. Its southern border with Kentucky is the Ohio River. Indiana has vast expanses of rural farmlands, yet it also has important manufacturing within its borders: steel making in the Chicago extension, automobile manufacturing in Kokomo, Anderson, and Muncie in central Indiana and in northeastern Fort Wayne; and power generation plants in the south.[2] Like Ohio, Indiana's eastern neighbor, the state's original settlers produced a split state culture that is bisected by Interstate 70: the northern half of the state was settled by Yankees, either from Ohio or directly from New England, while southerners from Kentucky and beyond moved into the state's southern half.[3] Southern and Eastern Europeans came to northwestern Gary area during the nineteenth and early twentieth century waves of immigration to work in its steel mills. With the exception of the Indiana extension of Chicago, Indiana is still populated "by descendants of its original settlers."[4]

Indiana's distinctive cultural division has produced a political culture that is currently typical of an earlier era in which party affiliation was controlled by Civil War events with some slight later effect from the Depression.[5] In Indiana, party dominance reflects early settlement patterns: the southern Indiana counties, where the early settlers were predominantly southerners, still vote Democratic; north of I-70, except in the northwest industrial corridor, the Yankee's descendants retain attachment to the Republican Party.[6] The voting behavior of Indianapolis, Indiana's largest metropolitan area, is similarly out of synch with present-day northern cities—it still votes strongly Republican, even against Democratic tides. This idiosyncratic political behavior is exhibited even in Indiana's auto manufacturing towns, Kokomo, Anderson, Muncie, and Fort Wayne. They continue to support Republican candidates at the top of the ticket.[7] Gary and the other cities in the northwest corridor are the Indiana exceptions; they vote overwhelmingly Democratic, even in Republican landslides.[8] In statewide races the major parties are competitive, perhaps because in Indiana Democratic statewide candidates run more conservative campaigns. Longtime Indiana political observers have noted that congressional Indiana liberals are much more conservative during election years. In recent presidential elections Indiana voters have given the state's electoral votes to the Republican candidate,[9] perhaps reflecting the state's underlying conservatism. Republican justices have been predominant on the Indiana court.[10]

THE INDIANA SUPREME COURT

Progressive History

The Indiana court has an impressive history of policy making. In 1991, the court's present chief justice, Randall Shepard, reviewed the conspicuous examples of his court's past in his forward to a review of progress in the law.[11] He described the Indiana court's championship of the humanity of the slaves and of the cause of their freedom from slavery at a time when other states' courts and the Supreme Court were basing their decisions on evaluations of slaves as property.[12] The Indiana court had defied legislative policy to require that the state pay lawyers who had been appointed to represent indigent defendants in criminal prosecution at a time when only two other states' courts (Iowa and Wisconsin) had done so.[13] The court ignored an implicit legislative disqualification of women to practice law and relied on its inherent control of the state's bar to admit women to the practice of law in Indiana.[14] Thirty-eight years before the Supreme Court excluded evidence obtained in an illegal search from a criminal prosecution, the Indiana court, in the face of adverse public opinion and contrary state laws, adopted that rule for admission of such evidence in the Indiana courts.[15]

Prominence and Decline

In 1885, when West Publishing Co. formed its judicial reporting regions, it joined Indiana with New York, Massachusetts, Michigan, and Ohio, whose courts were the leaders of the state benches at the time, in its prestigious Northeast reporting region.[16] Before 1910, the Indiana Supreme Court had been the fifth most cited supreme court in the country and in 1920 it was still the eighth most cited.[17] An uninterrupted decline of the court's reputation continued until 1975 when it had dropped to twenty-fifth in the country.[18] In 1989, Justice Shepard reviewed recent decisions by Indiana's sister courts and found that its decisions were being cited only by other Indiana courts. He observed that "we were writing to ourselves."[19]

By the beginning of the 1980s, the Indiana court showed no trace of the policy-making activism of its antislavery and feminist decisions. Prestige had evanesced and activism was somnolent. By contrast with the Indiana Supreme Court, the Indiana General Assembly, whose reputation was decidedly status quo, was more activist. A combination of relative legislative activism and court non-activism was achieved in a 1982 case in which the court gave a narrow restrictive interpretation to a legislative statute of limitations; this interpretation effectively eliminated workers' compensation protection for Indiana's asbestosis sufferers. The Indiana General Assembly responded immediately to the Indiana court's decision by clarifying its intention to provide protection for these industrial victims.[20]

The Indiana court's opportunity to make policy was somewhat narrowed by the Indiana Constitution, Article 7, Section 4, that provided: "Appeals from a judgment imposing a sentence of death, life imprisonment or imprisonment for a term greater than ten years shall be taken directly to the Supreme Court." This authority allowed the sentenced defendant to bypass review by the intermediate appellate court. Article 7, Section 4, had been adopted initially in 1970 when the addition of these criminal cases to the Indiana court's load by direct appeal was not oppressive. Legislative and sociological changes had generally increased the length of the sentences that were given to convicted felons with the result that by 1985 the Indiana court's docket was swamped by these convict's appeals. Measures that had increased the use of habitual offender statutes[21] had increased the number of defendants eligible for direct appeals to a court-crippling level. These mandatory criminal appeals in the lopsided caseload required the court to take increasingly more cases. In 1976, the Indiana court wrote only 137 of its opinions in cases on direct appeal. By 1985, 291 of the court's 313 opinions were written in these mandatory criminal appeal cases. In 1986, it issued almost two opinions per working day, "the highest number of opinions per (justice of any supreme court) in the country."[22] As a result, its discretionary docket was substantially curtailed and "many areas of the civil law go unaddressed."[23] An amendment to the Indiana Constitution, Proposition 2, proposed to change the appellate jurisdiction of the Indiana court to require it to automatically hear an appeal only if the prison term imposed was longer than fifty years. Justice Shepard wanted to regain the Indiana court's high reputation and recognized that deciding mandatory criminal cases sapped the court's energy. He worked diligently in the campaign to pass Proposition 2 and implored the Indiana Bar Association to work for its passage.[24]

Proposition 2 was adopted at the general election in November 1988 the Indiana court quickly adopted an implementing rule and the mix of the court's cases began to change. In 1985, 88 percent of its opinions had been written in mandatory criminal appeals. In 1990, opinions in these cases had fallen to 68 percent of those that it wrote. Table 2.1 illustrates these comparisons. One thread that had been running through the work of the Indiana court had been its "preoccupation . . . with criminal appeals."[25] The relief that the successful Proposition 2 campaign created eliminated this implied criticism. The reduction in the number of criminal appeals increased the opportunity for the Indiana court to consider a broader range of cases in which policy making is possible. The reduction of the criminal case burden gave it the opportunity to hear and decide important cases and the chance to achieve the promise of Shepard's vision.

Two institutional characteristics of the Indiana court system made it easier for the Indiana court to be a policy maker. Indiana had joined in the judicial reform

Table 2.1
Criminal Case Opinions in the Indiana Supreme Court, 1977–1990

YEAR	TOTAL OPINIONS	DIRECT CRIMINAL APPEAL OPINIONS	CIVIL TRANSFER OPINIONS
1990	206	**141 (68%)**	**51 (25%)**
1989	346	**286 (83%)**	**40 (12%)**
1988	306	**268 (88%)**	**23 (8%)**
1987	363	312 (86%)	32 (9%)
1986	445	395 (89%)	21 (5%)
1985	330	291 (88%)	22 (7%)
1984	327	280 (86%)	19 (6%)
1983	323	281 (87%)	24 (7%)
1982	334	285 (85%)	23 (7%)
1981	304	246 (81%)	38 (13%)
1980	270	226 (84%)	21 (8%)
1979	262	211 (80%)	21 (8%)
1978	275	234 (85%)	21 (8%)
1977	164	138 (84%)	12 (7%)

Source: The years 1976–1986 from *Res Gestae* 32: 56–57, p. 57; the years 1987–1990 from (1991) "Indiana Law, the Supreme Court, and a New Decade," *Indiana Law Review*, 24: 499–521, p. 501, note 7.

movement that had swept the United States in the 1960s and 1970s by adopting an amendment to its state constitution in 1970 that, among other changes, added an intermediate appellate court to the state judicial system[26] and a merit system for the selection of judges.[27] Both provisions, unlike the mandatory appeal of criminal cases, created conditions that could arguably enlarge the Indiana court's opportunity to make policy. The interposition of the intermediate appellate court provided the court with a filter that removed appeals in cases that demanded only routine examination and decision making from the system. The elimination of these cases from the stream of cases flowing to the Indiana court freed it from the burden of considering the everyday cases and allowed it to concentrate its time and energies on the more significant cases that posed alternative policy conclusions. The Indiana merit system for the selection of the state's appellate judges provided that after initial appointment by the governor, the judge served a ten-year term and had only to win a retention election to qualify for another ten-year term.[28] The ten-year term is substantially longer than the average term for a state high court justice in the United States and incumbent judges are retained in an overwhelming percent of retention election, elections in which the incumbent has no opposition.[29] The longer term and the likelihood that they will be retained freed the justices from any concern that their policy decisions would endanger their job security.

In Indiana the Judicial Nominating Commission was authorized to appoint the chief justice of the Indiana court for a five-year term from among the members of the court.[30] The chief justiceship is "subject to reappointment"[31] and Chief Justice Shepard was reappointed chief justice at the conclusion of his initial five-year term.

INDIANA JUDGES, 1980–1990

Justice Shepard

Randall Shepard was appointed to the Indiana Supreme Court bench in September 1985 to replace Justice Hunter. He was from a different mold than the other judges on the Indiana court. At thirty-nine he was the court's youngest member and, unlike other members, he had not been educated at a local Indiana law school but had graduated from Yale University Law School. Upon graduation he went to Washington, D.C., to serve as special assistant to the U.S. Secretary of Transportation. He became executive assistant to the mayor of Evansville on his return to Indiana in 1974 and later a candidate for mayor of his hometown. He had been appointed by the president of the United States to the Citizen Advisory Committee on Transportation Quality after his return to Indiana.

With the appointment of Randall Shepard to the court in September 1985, the merit selection had produced a justice with a strong belief in judicial activism and the likelihood that he would occupy a leadership position on the court. Shepard's legal education at a prestigious national law school qualified him, by default, as the intellectual leader of the court.[32] A legal education at a national law school will familiarize the lawyer with alternative solutions to problems that have been tried in various court systems and make the judge comfortable with the idea that there are a number of different solutions to any problem situation. A legal education at a local law school is more likely to have emphasized, to the exclusion of more progressive thinking, the solutions established by the local state's jurisprudence. Justice

Shepard's broader legal education and familiarity with a range of acceptable solutions to problems qualified him as a legitimate advocate of new ideas to his brethren on the bench and, from his elevated position, to the state bar.

The time he spent in political office prior to his ascension to the high court enabled him to both develop and appreciate the policy component of decision making. His public service and political candidacy had both been at the executive level where policy development was a requisite for the job. His appointment to the National Citizen's Advisory Committee was a high-level recognition of his interest and ability in policy development. Shepard's service in political office, particularly in the national government, would have been impressive to his brethren on the high court bench whose prejudicial professional backgrounds were small-town legal practices and attenuated service in the state legislature. His participation in the partisan Nixon administration at the subcabinet level could not have failed to impress the three other Republican members of the Indiana court.

Unlike the other members of the 1980s Indiana Supreme Court, Randall Shepard has written extensively, across a broad range of public policy issues: women's rights,[33] land use,[34] patriotism, abortion and the separation of church and state.[35] Shepard observed that when he had been appointed to the court, "the likelihood was that the court, in hearing a matter on the merits, would say of existing common law: 'That is the current law. If you wish to change it, go to the legislature.'"[36] He made clear his disagreement with this deferential role as well as the role he preferred the court to play in state government: "judges should not shrink from reexamination of traditional roles."[37]

His reluctance to defer to the legislature in matters of statutory policy making extended to a refusal to defer to the legislature or to past courts in matters of the judicially established common law: "I believe that *stare decisis*[38] is a helpful doctrine in the administration of justice, but it is not an end in itself,"[39] "judges should regard themselves as responsible for the rules they have erected."[40] In his first address to the Indiana Bar Association House of Delegates after his selection as chief justice, he prescribed: "The Indiana Supreme Court must start to write more civil law."[41] Shepard intended that the "civil law" that the court was to write would be innovative and current. Shortly after his appointment to the court, a former Yale Law School professor advised him: "If you have not touched a subject since 1940 . . . and all you do now is what others did in 1960, you may miss the opportunity to correct the mistakes of 1960. You have to find new solutions."[42] Shepard obviously appreciated this advice.

When Randall Shepard went to the court in 1985, he prescribed an activist role for it. At that time he was concerned about the court's reputation and prestige. After only six years on the court he was able to note, in 1992, that cases that the court had decided since 1985 had been cited by other state high courts sixty-three times.[43] Shepard was clearly alluding to his earlier observation that the court had been "writing to ourselves." Indiana's sister courts had recognized the change in the importance of its decision making and were again using its decisions to help them to decide their cases. The Indiana court had become a current and significant judicial voice. The rapid reversal of the fortunes of the Indiana court coincided with Shepard's advocacy of an active, policy-making role for the court. He has recognized and approved "the aspirations of state court judges to be independent sources of the law."[44] After serving a little more than a decade as the chief justice of the Indiana court, he examined traditional judicial decision making and compared it with that of the current role preferences of the Indiana justices and concluded that these preferences have changed from those of the early 1980s: "The classic image of the judge" is that "Courts . . . decide how . . . policies made by others should be applied." This "rigid focus on 'applying the law' can readily become narrowness of vision." This is not "what Indiana judges were about in 1997."[45]

A change occurred in the support for activist, policy-making decisions from a minority to a majority immediately after the appointment of Randall Shepard to the Indiana court. At the time of his appointment only one of the other judges had given any evidence of an activist bent, Justice DeBruler. Shepard replaced the other justice with activist potential, Justice Hunter. When Shepard replaced Hunter, his vote combined with DeBruler's created only a minority on the five-member court and yet, from the time of his appointment, activism was the dominant role when the court was in a position to make policy and Justice Shepard was a member of the majority in every activist decision. The activist promise of his educational, professional, and political background was confirmed by his speeches and writing immediately upon his appointment. His written opinions as a member of the court regularly considered the policy ramifications of the alternatives before the court, which was a substantial departure from the formalistic opinions that had been *de riguer* for the Indiana court prior to his appointment. Although Shepard's tenure on the court has not been without personal tension,[46] it hasn't diminished Shepard's ability to lead the Indiana court's decision making. In a recent five year period he was "in the majority more than any other member."[47]

Other Members of the Indiana Court

Neither the educational nor professional pre-court experiences of the justices who were on the court in 1985 would have nourished a policy-making spirit and their writings, neither before nor after ascending the high bench, contain no hint of budding activism.[48] Each had graduated from an Indiana law school. Justice DeBruler had briefly been an Indianapolis deputy city prosecutor and had served on various lower courts before his appointment to the court in 1968. He was the lone Democrat on the court during the 1980s. Justice DeBruler had not written anything that was published outside his judicial duties. Justice Prentice and Justice Pivarnik had both practiced law in small Indiana communities before being elevated to the bench and neither had any extra-judicial writing that was published. Justice Hunter had similarly practiced law in a small town and had served one two-year term in the state legislature. He had published two essays in professional journals that supported legal reform, but neither essay advocated judicial policy making to achieve the reforms he supported.

The chief justice, Richard Givan, had practiced law in Indianapolis and had served one term in the state legislature before his election to the court in 1969. The chief had the most extensive writing experience of the members of the court in 1985, but this was the result of the obligatory annual reviews of judicial activity that bar associations and state law school reviews expect of state supreme court chief justices. None of these routine writing assignments contain an explanation of his judicial philosophy except, significantly, an admonition that the judges' oaths require them to "refrain from transgressing into the proper functions" of the legislative and executive branches.[49]

There is nothing in the backgrounds or experiences of these justices whom Randall Shepard joined in September 1985 that would predict that any of them would upset established applecarts. There is no evidence that any of them advocated active judicial policy making. There was only one addition to the court during the decade after Shepard joined it in 1985, Justice Brent E. Dickson. Dickson had practiced law in Lafayette, Indiana, a city of approximately 40,000, until his appointment to the court and had written two articles for professional journals while in private practice, each describing a specific area of the practice of law, but neither of which examined either the policy antecedents or consequences of the state of the law in the particular area.

INDIANA SUPREME COURT CASES, 1980–1990

1980–1985, Non-Activist Cases

A combination of legislative activism and restrained judicial decision making was achieved in Indiana in a 1982 case in which the Indiana court's decision gave a restrictive interpretation to a legislative statute of limitations that eliminated workers' compensation protection for Indiana's asbestosis sufferers. The Indiana General Assembly responded immediately to the Indiana court's decision by emphasizing its intention to provide protection.[50]

During the first half of the 1980s, practicing Indiana lawyers maintained a drumbeat of criticism of the Indiana court. They charged that, rather than acting independently, it had subordinated itself to the general assembly. A specialist in personal injury law observed that the Indiana Torts Claims Act was given a "restrictive interpretation . . . in a way sharply limiting claimant's rights." He charged that the Indiana court's decisions in products liability cases "seem to be a result of complete deference to the legislature."[51] Criticism of the Indiana court continued during this period and sharpened in 1984: "In relation to the traditional goals of tort law . . . Indiana has taken giant strides backwards in time. . . . In support of its protective policy . . . (it) has relied upon discredited and outdated rationales."[52]

The court was not unanimous in the restrained, traditional approach to policy making that its critics had described. In addition to the criticism by the gown and bar of the court's subservience to the legislature, another pattern that emerged during this period was the dissents of Justices DeBruler and Hunter from the court's non-activist decisions. These joined dissents from the Indiana court's restrained decision making suggest that this minority of the members of the Indiana court was willing to make policy. Although their disagreements with the majority in cases in which the court refused to make change is apparent, it is doubtful that the source of this disagreement was an attachment to the activist judicial role. There is little in the backgrounds or nonjudicial writings of either justice to suggest that he had a particular interest in judicial policy making or judicial independence. To the contrary, Justice DeBruler's call for help to the legislature in his dissent in the court's second nude dancing case is evidence of his satisfaction with the court's deferential role. Any activist inclination these justices may have had in the early 1980s was, at most, incipient. However, their regular disagreement with the refusal by the early 1980s court to join the state's policy makers signaled their potential enlistment in the ranks of an activist advocate.

Abortion. The Indiana Courts of Appeal had marched into the thicket of abortion-related regulation and had held that an Indiana law that required an abortion clinic to be licensed was unconstitutional under the Indiana Constitution. The restrained Indiana court would not touch the case.[53]

Products Liability Cases. The Indiana Courts of Appeal made fifteen intentional activist policy decisions in the area of products liability during late 1979 and early 1980,[54] and when each of these cases was appealed to the Indiana court, it refused the policy-making challenge to change the course of common-law products liability doctrine or legislative policy. It either refused to hear the case on appeal or reversed the court of appeals on narrow procedural grounds.

The Common Law. The question of the legal duty of third parties[55] was a hot one during the 1980s. In this area of the law the Indiana Courts of Appeal intrepidly made policy, holding that those who gratuitously undertake to render service are liable if they fail and, in a related area of the law, that a host has a duty to control a guest in order to protect another guest. The Indiana court backed away from both policy issues.[56] One court of appeals had been doubly active in a volunteer case by setting aside a legislative act that had provided that there was no affirmative duty to act to protect another and then by judicially adopting as the common law of Indiana the rule[57] that one who has gratuitously undertaken to render service to another is liable for failure to render such service.[58] The Indiana court refused to hear an appeal from this decision, so the new doctrine was controlling only in the limited geographic jurisdiction of the court of appeals and even there without the imprimatur of the Indiana court. Another court of appeals departed from the traditional common-law principle that one does not have a duty to control the conduct of another and found that a host has a duty to control the conduct of one guest in order to prevent injury to another guest. The Indiana court considered the appeal in this case only to reverse the court of appeals, thereby returning the law to the traditional common-law policy.[59]

Criminal Cases. During most of the 1980s, the Indiana court's docket was overwhelmed by criminal appeals, but the number of its decisions in these cases did not produce progressive or enlightened decisions. Constitutional protection for nude dancing in public was a recurring issue during the 1980s in Indiana as it was throughout the United States. The court repeatedly deferred to the legislature when the validity of legislative prohibition was questioned. In 1979, the court had held that nude dancing in bars and taverns was not protected by the U.S. Constitution's First Amendment.[60] Justices DeBruler and Hunter had disagreed and dissented. In 1984, an Indiana Court of Appeals noted that there was a recent line of U.S. Supreme Court cases that suggested that the First Amendment protected nude dancing[61] and, based on the reasoning of those cases, it held that nude dancing was constitutionally protected expression. This case arose at a time when activist state supreme courts were beginning to take the unusual step of using their states' constitutions as independent sources of protection of civil rights in their states in the face of the U.S. Supreme Court's narrowing interpretations of the individual's rights protected by the U.S. Constitution.[62] The Indiana court would not even take advantage of *favorable* U.S. Supreme Court decisions to protect the citizens of Indiana from a state statute that was "incurably overbroad in regulating expression protected by the first amendment."[63] In deciding the appeal from the court of appeals decision, the Indiana court used only five paragraphs to reaffirm its holding in its 1979 case.[64] Justice De Bruler and Hunter continued their earlier dissent. Significantly, for the state of judicial activism in the Indiana court at the time, De Bruler's dissenting opinion preferred "a remand to the legislature to . . . draw the line between legitimate public nudity and criminal public nudity."[65]

1985–1990, Return to Policy Making

The court's decisions in product liability, abortion, third-party liability, and nude dancing cases exemplify the court's pervasive restrained judicial role during this period toward making policy change.[66] It was also a period before the Indiana court was relieved of the heavy burden of criminal appeals. However, the court did not wait until its criminal docket was lightened to turn from the non-activism of the early 1980s. In December 1985, less than three months after Randall Shepard joined the Indiana court, it made its first significant activist decision of the decade. The Indiana Public Service Corporation had allowed a utility to include the costs of closing plants in its rate-making formula. A number of nuclear generating plants around the country had to be closed as a result of citizen protest campaigns during the late 1970s and early 1980s and utilities companies had tried to pass these close-down costs to their customers. In Indiana, the regulatory agency, the Public Service Corporation, had approved consumer rates that included these close-down costs according to the traditional formula that had been implicitly approved by the Indiana legislature. In this first important activist decision of the decade, the court reversed these legislatively approved interpretations of the Public Service Corporation and eliminated nuclear close-down costs from the utility bills. Justice DeBruler wrote the court's opinion and was joined by Justices Shepard and Pivarnik.[67]

During the remaining years of the 1980s, the Indiana court reached ten other intentional activist results. These eleven decisions in the slightly more than four years was a significant increase over the two that the court had reached in the decade's first six years. The Indiana court swept away rules and doctrine that had blocked efforts of the injured to be compensated for their injuries. It adopted a progressive rule for Indiana trial courts to use in selecting the law to apply in tort cases when there were conflicting foreign states' laws. In a remarkable burst of common-law activity the court created five new common law causes of action and suggested a sixth in a related workers' compensation case.

Common Law, Elimination of Restrictive Doctrine. Previous Indiana court decisions had affirmed the doctrine of sovereign immunity and defined it to protect governments from liability for injury caused by all governmental decision. The post-1985 court switched the prevailing emphasis; governments would be liable for all decisions except those that involved "fundamental policy."[68] An earlier court had held that a person injured by the state's action could not sue the state unless the claimant notified the state attorney general *even though the Attorney General already knew.*[69] The court, in an opinion by Justice Dickson in which Justices Shepard and DeBruler joined, swept away this long-standing and formalistic interpretation of the notice statute and concluded that the policy behind the notice statute was to allow prompt investigation of claims and that this policy was served by "substantial, if not actual, compliance."[70]

Conflict of Laws.[71] Over one hundred years of precedent in the Indiana court had established that Indiana courts would apply the law of the state in which a tort occurred in a trial in Indiana of the resulting cause of action. The new court overruled this body of cases[72] and adopted the modern rule[73] that required the trial court to apply the law of the state having the "most significant contacts" with the tort and the parties to the action.

Common Law, New Causes of Action. The Indiana court considered six cases in which it was requested to approve new causes of action and it approved five of them. In the sixth case, the court demonstrated that it was truly an activist court although the court decided not to overturn the common-law doctrine.

In the first of these cases, the recently reinvigorated court disregarded a legislative act and overruled an earlier case in order to allow a traffic victim to bring an action against a "dramshop" operator. In 1984, the court had held that because the legislature had enacted a criminal statute that prohibited a bar owner from selling an alcoholic beverage to a customer who was known to be intoxicated, there could be no common-law action against the bar owner for injuries caused by the intoxicated customer.[74] Just four years later[75] the court overruled its earlier decision and found that the injured party had a common law cause of action that was separate and independent of the statutory law.

Next, a unanimous Shepard court carved out an exception to the common law rule that an employer may discharge for any reason an employee who does not have a contract and recognized a new cause of action against an employer who had discharged an employee in retaliation for that employee's refusal to commit an illegal act.[76] It was necessary for the court to overrule a 107-year-old case that had absolved Indiana landlords from any duty to make repairs to leased premises in order to recognize the next new cause of action for Indiana tenants. The unanimous court adopted the modern rule[77] that a tenant has a cause of action against a landlord for injury caused by the landlord's failure to repair premises that the landlord had agreed to repair.[78] In the fourth case, the court found that a child who had been sexually assaulted by employees of an institution in whose care the child had been entrusted had a cause of action against the institution for the sexual assault by its employees.[79] In a workers' compensation case, the court departed from the traditional rule that a claim for mental injury that was not accompanied by a physical injury could not be compensated.[80] The Indiana civil law did not recognize a similar cause of action for mental injury without physical injury and this workers' compensation decision might presage a similar decision in the civil law.[81]

Chief Justice Shepard crafted an opinion that created a new common law doctrine in an important area of commercial law. Prior to Shepard's opinion, the Indiana commercial law of the proof of commercial agreements was a conservative one that did not allow the parties to describe a written agreement in court.[82] Justice Shepard, writing for the court, emasculated this traditional rule and allowed the parties to explain their agreement as part of their case.[83]

The distance along the road of activism that the Indiana court had traveled during the five years since September 1985 is demonstrated in an opinion in a case in 1990 in which it had an opportunity to establish a new common law cause of action for a child's loss of parent's services, society, and companionship.[84] Justice Dickson, writing for the court, reviewed the policy considerations that militated for the alternate decisions and concluded that this policy review warranted against allowing the action. However, the court did not believe that this policy question should be left to the legislature. "We find the question whether the common law should recognize a child's action for loss of parental consortium to be entirely *appropriate for judicial determination*."[85] The court had faced the question of the propriety of a judicial determination whether a cause of action should be created and had decided that it was not only proper but preferable to a legislative determination. Although the court's decision did not result in a change in Indiana policy, that decision was made by a court that recognized activism as an acceptable role. It had come a long way from 1982 when it "would not infringe on the legislature's sole responsibility."[86]

NOTES

*An earlier version of this chapter was included in *Indiana Politics and Public Policy*, Maurice Eisenstein, ed. (Needham Heights, Mass.: Simon and Schuster, 1999), pp. 111–127, and is included here by permission.

1. Michael Barone and Grant Ujifusa, *Almanac of American Politics 1996* (Washington, D.C.: National Journal, 1995), p. 468.

2. Barone and Ujifusa, *1996*, pp. 467, 468.

3. Barone and Ujifusa, *1996*, p. 467.

4. Barone and Ujifusa, *1996*, p. 468.

5. Michael Barone and Grant Ujifusa, *Almanac of American Politics 1994* (Washington, D.C.: National Journal, 1993), p. 435.

6. Barone and Ujifusa, *1994*, pp. 435–436.

7. Barone and Ujifusa, *1994*, p. 436.

8. Barone and Ujifusa, *1994*, p. 436.

9. Barone and Ujifusa, *1996,* p. 468.

10. Indiana adopted a merit system for selecting its court's justices in 1970 and since that year justices have been initially appointed by the governor, subject to a public retention vote every ten years. The political affiliation of the justice initially appointed has matched that of the appointing governor.

11. The Hon. Randall T. Shepard, "Indiana Law and the Idea of Progress," *Indiana Law Review* 25 (1992): 943–956.

12. *Donnell v. State*, 3 Ind. 480 (1852).

13. *Webb v. Baird*, 6 Ind. 14 (1854).

14. *In re Leach*, 34 N.E. 641 (1893).

15. *Callendar v. State*, 138 N.E. 817 (1923).

16. Rodney L. Mott, "Judicial Influence," *American Political Review* 30 (1936): 295–315, p. 308.

17. Mott, "Judicial Influence," p. 308.

18. Gregory Caldeira, "On the Reputation of State Courts," *Political Behavior* 5 (1983): 83.

19. The Hon. Randall T. Shepard, "State of the Judiciary: In Search of Excellence," *Res Gestae* 33 (Mar. 1990): 421–424.

20. *Bunker v. National Gypsum Company*, 441 N.E.2d 8 (1982). Asbestosis is a condition that can be caused by inhalation of asbestos fiber and gradually develops over a number of years. It does not cause noticeable symptoms until it has progressed at least ten years; restrictive statutes of limitations would have run out before symptoms appear. "Survey of Recent Developments in Indiana Law," *Indiana Law Review* 19(1986): 35, citing *Gray's Attorneys Textbook of Medicine*, paragraph 205,C.30.

21. Statutes that make it a criminal offense to have been convicted of crimes prior to the immediate offense that led to trial. The penalty for habitual offender status crimes is greater than for any single offense

22. The Hon. Randall T. Shepard, "Vote Yes on Proposition 2 or 'I'm Sorry, But There's No Supreme Court Case on That,'" *Res Gestae* 32 (1988): 56.

23. Shepard, "Vote Yes," pp. 56–57.

24. Shepard, "Vote Yes," pp. 56–57.

25. E. Matthew Neff, "Constitutional Law," *Indiana Law Review* 15 (1982): 157.

26. Constitution of the State of Indiana, Art VII, Sec. 5.

27. Constitution of the State of Indiana, Art VII, Sec. 10.

28. Constitution of the State of Indiana, Art. VII, Sec. 10.

29. Lawrence Baum, *American Courts*, third ed. (Boston: Houghton Mifflin, 1994), p. 126, and Christopher E. Smith, *Courts, Politics, and the Judicial Process* (Chicago: Nelson-Hall, 1993), p. 108.

30. Constitution of the State of Indiana, Art. 7, Sec. 3.

31. Constitution of the State of Indiana, Art. 7, Sec. 3.

32. Doug Sword, "Ten Years at the Top," Gary, Indiana *Post-Tribune*, September 10, 1995, p. E1, in which Sword quotes Kevin Betz, author of a study done for the *Indiana Law Review*: "Clearly he's the one most able to be the leader of the Court intellectually."

33. The Hon. Randall T. Shepard, "A Bill of Rights for the Whole Nation," *Valparaiso University Law Review* 26 (Fall, 1991): 27–35.

34. The Hon. Randall T. Shepard, "Land Use Regulation in the Rehnquist Court: The Fifth Amendment and Judicial Intervention," *Catholic University Law Review* 38 (Summer, 1989): 847–869.

35. The Hon. Randall T. Shepard, "Flag Burning, Abortions, and the Creche: the Role of the Supreme Court in Governing America," *Res Gestae* 33 (January, 1990): 315–318.

36. "State Court Widens Its Focus," The Fort Wayne, Indiana, *The News Sentinel*, December 3, 1990, p. 5A.

37. "New Chief Justice Outlines Agenda for State's Judiciary," *Res Gestae* 30 (June, 1987): 5.

38. "The principle that past decisions should stand as precedents for future decisions." Otis H. Stephens and John M. Scheb, II, *American Constitutional Law* (Minneapolis/St. Paul, Minn.: West Publishing Company, 1993) p. D–15.

39. "New Chief Justice Outlines."

40. *Miller v. Mayberry*, 506 N.E.2d 7 (1987), p. 11. Justice Shepard refused to join the court's opinion and wrote a concurring opinion that made clear his disagreement with the court's stated position that change in the wrongful death doctrine *that the Court had initially formulated* must come from the legislature.

41. "New Chief Justice Outlines"

42. Advice to Justice Shepard from his Yale University Law School professor, E. Donald Elliott. The Hon. Randall T. Shepard, "Indiana and the Idea of Progress," *Indiana Law Review* 25 (1992): 943–956.

43. Shepard, "Indiana and the Idea."

44. The Hon. Randall T. Shepard, "The Maturing Nature of State Constitution Jurisprudence," *Valparaiso University Law review* 30 (Spring, 1996): 421–457.

45. The Hon. Randall T. Shepard, "Indiana Courts as Servants of Their Communities," his annual address to the Indiana General Assembly, January 14, 1998.

46. See Sword, "Ten Years."

47. Sword, "Ten Years."

48. The justices' biographic information is found in various entries in various editions of *The American Bench, Judges of the Nation.*

49. The Hon. Richard M. Givan, "Indiana—The State of the Judiciary," *Res Gestae* 26 (1983): 429.

50. *Bunker v. National Gypsum Company*, 441 N.E.2d 8 (1982). State courts in other states have adopted rules that have modified legislative statutes of limitations to avoid unfair application to those affected by slowly developing medical conditions such as asbestosis. See *O'Stricker v. Jim Walter Corp.*, 447 N.E.2d 727 (1983), Ohio.

51. John F. Vargo, "Products Liability," *Indiana Law Review* 14 (1982): 1–64.

52. John F. Vargo, "Torts," *Indiana Law Review* 17 (1984): 341–385.

53. *Indiana Hospital Licensing Council v. Women's Pavilion of South Bend*, 420 N.E. 2d 1031 (1982).

54. Jordan H. Lieberman, "Products Liability." *Indiana Law Review* 14 (1981): 1–64.

55. Parties not directly involved in an injury.

56. *Perry v. Northern Indiana Service Company*, 433 N.E. 2d 44 (1982) and *Martin v. Sheen*, 463 N.E. 2d 1092 (1984).

57. See *Restatement of Torts*, Section 324.

58. *Perry v. Northern Indiana Service Company*, 433 N.E. 2d 44 (1982).

59. *Martin v. Sheen*, 463 N.E. 2d 1092 (1984). Justice De Bruler disagreed and dissented.

60. Justices De Bruler and Hunter had disagreed with the majority and had dissented.

61. See *Schad v. Borough of Mt. Ephraim*, 452 U.S. 61 (1981).

62. Ronald L. K. Collins, Peter J. Gailie, and John Kincaid, "State Courts, State Court Constitutions, and Individual Rights Litigation Since 1980: A Judicial Survey," *Publius* 16 (Vol. 3, 1986): 141–161.

63. "Survey of Recent Developments in Indiana Law," *Indiana Law Review* 19 (1986): 1.

64. *Erhardt v. State*, 468 N.E.2d 224 (1984).

65. *Erhardt,* p. 226.

66. However, in the period January 1, 1980 to September 8, 1985, there were two decisions that would qualify as activist. In both cases the court declared an act of the general assembly invalid: it declared Indiana's Occupational Income Tax unconstitutional because it discriminated against non-residents who earned income in Indiana, *Clark v. Lee* 406 N.E.2d 646 (1981), and it held invalid a legislative act that allowed both the state and the criminal defendant an automatic change of judges because it conflicted with the court's similar rule, *State, ex el. Jeffries v. Lawrence Circuit Court, et al.*, 467 N.E.2d 741 (1984). With the exception of these small oases of activism, the first half of the 1980s was barren.

67. *Citizens Action Coalition of Indiana, Inc. v. Northern Indiana Public Service Company, et al.*, 485 N.E.2d 610 (1985). Chief Justice Givan and Justice Prentice dissented charging that "rate making is a legislative and not a judicial function."

68. *Peavler v. Monroe County Board of Commissioners*, 528 N.E.2d 40 (1988).

69. *Geyer v. City of Loganport*, 377 N.E.2d 333 (1977).

70. *Indiana State Highway Commission v. Morris, et al.*, 528 N.E.2d 468 (1988). Chief Justice Givan and Justice Pivarnik continued to look to the legislature for any changed direction in statutory policy.

71. Conflict of laws is the body of rules that courts apply to determine which state law to apply in a case in which the residence of the parties and the place in which the activity giving rise to the case are not identical.

72. *Hubbard Manufacturing Co. v. Greeson*, 515 N.E.2d 1071 (1987).

73. *Restatement (Second) of Conflicts of Laws*, Section 145 (1971).

74. *Whisman v. Fawcett*, 470 N.E.2d 73 (1984).

75. *Piccadilly, Inc. v. Colvey*, 519 N.E.2d 1217 (1988). Justice Pivarnik, in dissent, sounded the complaint of the stubborn non-activists: "Where the legislature has established the standard of care required, the court cannot apply common law principles."

76. *McClanaghan v. Remington Freight Lines*, 517 N.E.2d 390 (1988).

77. *Restatement (Second) of Torts*.

78. *Childress v. Bowser*, 546 N.E.2d 1221 (1989).

79. *Stropes et al. v. Heritage House, etc., et al.*, 547 N.E.2d 244 (1990). The imposition of this duty on an institution to protect children from this kind of attack was a "wide sweeping change" and Justices Givan and Pivarnik dissented, repeating their claim that the legislature should make such changes.

80. *Hansen v. Duprin*, 507 N.E.2d 573 (1986).

81. See Carolyn Spangler, "Hansen v. Duprin: Have the Floodgates Opened to Workmen's Compensation Claims?," *Indiana Law Review* 21 (1988): 453.

82. This is the traditional "parol evidence" rule.

83. *Travel Craft v. William Mende, etc.*, 552 N.E.2d 443 (1990). Shepard ruled that a party to a written agreement may explain a written agreement that is incomplete in any respect. Since virtually no written commercial agreement is a complete statement of every term of the agreement between the parties, this decision leaves the parol evidence rule with no practical application. This opinion effectively eliminated the anti-consumer parol evidence rule and established common-law doctrine in an important area of commercial law that had previously been controlled by statute. Justice Givan found himself part of this activist court majority, although he had been in the non-activist majority in the next previous parol evidence decision that the court had overruled in *Travel Craft*. After *Travel Craft* every member of the Indiana court had embraced activism at least once since 1985.

84. *Dearborn Fabricating and Engineering Corp., Inc. v. Wickham*, 551 N.E.2d 1135 (1990). In the eight states that have recognized this cause of action it is known as parental consortium. Twenty-three states have refused to recognize it.

See *Villareal v. State Department of Transportation*, 774 P.2d 213 (Ariz. 1989).
    85. *Dearborn*, at p. 1136.
    86. *Bunker v. National Gypsum Co.*, 441 N.E.2d 8 (1982).

Chapter 3

West Virginia

West Virginia is one of the Civil War border states, states that had a substantial slave population at the start of the war but remained in the Union. Unlike the other border states, the area that is now West Virginia was part of Virginia but did not have a substantial slave population nor did it remain a part of the Union after the war began, yet split from Virginia during the war.[1] Present day West Virginia was the western mountain counties of Virginia that left the Union as part of Virginia before the war. It wasn't until the middle of the war, 1863, that these western counties broke away from Virginia, formed a separate state and were admitted to the Union as the State of West Virginia. It lies at the juncture of the East, South, and Midwest but is not much like any of them. It is most similar to the anomalous regions of eastern Ohio and western Pennsylvania with its economic activity narrowly concentrated in the basic coal and steel industries. West Virginia's economic health reflects the fortunes of these industries just as does that of its neighbors. The state's economy is dependent on coal, steel, and chemicals and its long-running depression reflects these industries' declining importance.[2] The settlers of pre-statehood West Virginia were Virginians and later newcomers came from the adjoining Appalachian area to work in West Virginia's southern coal mines during the boom years between 1880 and 1920.[3] In the mid and late nineteenth century, Eastern and Southern Europeans came to work in these coal mines[4] as well as to West Virginia's Northern Panhandle to man its steel mills, just as they came to neighboring eastern Ohio and western Pennsylvania.

In presidential politics, West Virginia is one of the most Democratic states; its voters give the state's electoral votes to the Republican candidate only in Republican landslide years.[5] But there are areas of West Virginia that have remained staunchly Republican since the Civil War: some sparsely populated mountain counties, cities and towns along the Ohio River and the Charleston-Kanawha Valley, the state's most populous area. These pockets of Republican strength are the state's political legacy from the Civil War and its attachment to the Union at the time of its admission.[6] The southern coalfields, the counties south of Charleston, received a different and more recent political inheritance. These counties are "one of the most Democratic parts of the nation," a legacy of the New Deal and the area's unionization during the 1930's.[7] Surprisingly, in view of the state's support for Democratic presidential candidates, in recent years the parties have alternated control of the governor's mansion; West Virginia voters have chosen two Republicans, Arch Moore and Cecil Underwood, and two Democrats, Jay Rockefeller and Hugh Caperton. Since 1968, the rival champions, Moore and Rockefeller, have dominated gubernatorial politics while Caperton and Underwood are the most recent incumbents.[8] Except for Republicans who have been appointed to fill vacancies by Republican governors, the West Virginia court has been dominated by Democratic justices.

THE WEST VIRGINIA SUPREME COURT OF APPEALS

Traditional History

The West Virginia Supreme Court of Appeals, West Virginia's highest court, was historically a conservative court that was "passiv(e) in matters of public policy."[9] This reputation is confirmed by separate studies of its level of innovation and of its reputation, respectively, among the other state courts. The West Virginia court ranked forty-sixth among the state courts in a study of trends in tort law innovation between 1945 and 1975.[10] Other state courts had little respect for the West Virginia court's opinions. It ranked forty-third in reputation among the state courts for the year 1975 measured by the frequency with which its opinions were cited by the other state courts.[11] Although neither innovation nor reputation is the same as activism, in a period of doctrinal innovation the similarity of a state court's rank for innovation and its rank for citation is a rough gauge of the level of its independent policy making or activism. The combined rankings of the West Virginia court describe a conservative court that was mired in inferiority.

During the period 1930 to 1977, the West Virginia court was conservative in tort and worker's compensation cases and deferential to the other branches of state government.[12] The traditional West Virginia court began to change its direction as a result of the 1972 judicial election. In the 1972 election there were contests for two seats on the West Virginia court that were occupied by justices who had been appointed by a Republican governor, an exception in this preponderantly Democratic state. The Republican incumbents were beaten by their Democratic challengers, Richard Neely and James Sprouse. The 1972 judicial election was exceptional for another reason: it had made the initial selection of two new justices for the West Virginia court. In the previous forty years, only two other justices had been selected initially by election.[13]

A consideration of recent activism in the West Virginia court is divided naturally into two distinct, though contiguous periods, 1973–1977 and 1977–1986. Prior to Richard Neely's election in 1972, the West Virginia court was a "stagnant," deferential, and conservative court that did not participate in making its state's governmental policy.[14] In 1972, the year before Neely joined the court, it had refused to reconsider the established West Virginia common law doctrine that those who use dangerous instruments in their business are not liable for injuries they cause unless they have been negligent.[15] Neely had no difficulty in avoiding that traditional doctrine when he "found" that West Virginia law makes a manufacturer who is engaged in a dangerous activity strictly liable to one who is injured by it in the absence of the manufacturer's negligence.[16] During the first four years of Neely's tenure on the court, it overruled earlier cases that had established significant policy in the areas of workers' compensation,[17] personal injury law (tort),[18] and criminal procedure[19] that had been decided by earlier courts. It also decided three cases that grew out of a budget dispute that had arisen between the state's Republican governor and its Democratically controlled legislature.[20] Although overruling court-made common law precedents and establishing policy where none had previously existed requires a lower threshold of activism than declaring legislatively established policy invalid, the West Virginia court was taking a significant first step for a court that had previously ignored any policy-making role.[21]

The Republican governor continued in office until early 1977 and after the 1972 election he filled two more high court vacancies with Republican judges.[22] Both these seats were contested in the 1976 election, along with a third seat that was occupied by a retiring Democrat. All three of these 1976 contests were won by the Democratic candidates, Sam Harshbarger, Darrel McGraw, and Thomas Miller. These judges joined Democrat judges Richard Neely, who had won in 1972, and Fred Caplan, who had been first appointed to the court in 1962.[23]

Policy Making Departure

The 1976 election not only returned the court to unanimous Democratic control, it also accomplished a shift in the court's judicial philosophy along with "one of the most momentous transfers of power in the state's history,"[24] the consequences of which were "found throughout the state."[25] The court's reputation as a conservative and deferential court was about to change to a reputation "for dramatic intervention in public policy disputes."[26] An oft-quoted feature article on the West Virginia court in the state capitol's leading newspaper, the Charleston *Gazette*, described things to come: "West Virginia's activist Supreme Court kept trying to mold state government in its own image in 1983. The Court issued decisions making or reinterpreting law across a wide expanse of public issues."[27] After the judicial election of 1976, the court began a period of vigorous activism; it continued to reexamine and change the court-made common law, sometimes going considerably farther than its most progressive peers in establishing new doctrine; it created new rules when unique circumstances required; it became the final arbiter of policy disputes between the other branches of West Virginia's government; and it intrepidly disagreed with the legislature.

In 1979, the court won the Outstanding Appellate Court Award that is made annually by the American Trial Lawyers Association, an organization of plaintiffs' lawyers. An association of plaintiffs' lawyers would be expected to reserve its highest praise for activist judicial behavior. The court's judicial conservatism and deference were, in 1979, things of the past. In 1988, a reporter for a national legal newspaper reviewed the result of the court's metamorphosis and concluded that the "court (had) wrought great changes in once-stagnant West Virginia law and pulled it into—and in some cases ahead of—the mainstream."[28]

Table 3.1 is a comparison of the levels at which the court exhibited behavior consistent with judicial activism. This table contrasts the levels of activist behavior before and after the wellspring judicial elections of 1972 and 1976. The substantial increase in the overall level of activism after 1976 ("A-Level"), the significantly high levels at which the court disregarded its established common law during the period 1973 to 1976 ("A-Precedent"), and the extent it relied on the state constitution, rather than the U.S. Constitution, during the period 1977 through 1985 (A-Constitution) show the significant increase in the West Virginia court's policy making after the judicial election in 1972.

Table 3.1
Levels of Activism in the West Virginia Supreme Court of Appeals, 1930–1985

PERIOD	MEAN N	A-LEVEL[1]	A-PRECEDENT[2]	A-CONSTITUTION[3]
1930-1937	231	.194	.031	.094
1938-1941	183	.127	.000	.000
1942-1952	108	.185	.000	.048
1953-1958	73	.204	.143	.143
1959-1972	76	.318	.107	.107
1973-1976	90	.139	**.667**	.000
1977-1985	211	**.421**	.185	**.296**

[1] A-Level is proportion of activist cases to total cases.
[2] A-Precedent is proportion of activist cases that overrule precedent.
[3] A-Constitution is proportion of activist cases that rely on the West Virginia Constitution.
Source: Hagan, "Policy Activism."[29]

The January 1, 1984, Charleston *Gazette* article noted that the court's activism played in a broad range of issue areas, encompassing social welfare, education, criminal law, women's rights, consumerism, and intergovernmental relations.[30] In addition to the areas that the newspaper found interesting, the Court also manifested activism in the development of common-law doctrine, particularly in tort/workers' compensation law.

There were no structural changes in the West Virginia court or judicial system during the period 1977 to 1986. The system is an unreformed traditional state court system. West Virginia is one of a minority of states that does not have an intermediate appellate court between its trial courts and its high court. However, it is the only state high court that has absolute control of its docket.[31] Unlike the Indiana court that, before the November 1988 election was required to hear the appeals of the vast majority of convicted criminal defendants, the West Virginia court hears only those cases it wants to decide. Despite this control, its docket ballooned during the period 1976 to 1986. In 1976, the court had heard and written opinions in ninety-eight cases while by 1986 the number of opinions it wrote had increased to 213.[32] Ordinarily, a more than 100 percent increase in the level of court activity in a ten-year period would cause a diminution of the court's effort and time available for policy-making decisions. However, the increased activity when joined with absolute control over its docket suggests that the court took the additional cases it decided for the purpose of making state policy.

Unlike the appointed Indiana court, the judges of the West Virginia court are elected in statewide partisan elections after they have been nominated in party primaries. Their twelve-year terms[33] are among the longest for the state courts with definite terms. The West Virginia Constitution authorizes the members of the court to select the court's chief justice.[34] The judges have caused the chief justiceship to rotate annually among the court's five judges, which has allowed each judge at least two, separated, one-year periods as chief during the course of each 12-year term.

During the period 1977 to 1987, the West Virginia court was dominated by Democratic judges and that domination was total. With the exception of the last two years of the period when one new Democratic judge joined the court, its membership was unchanged. Similarly, during the entire period the governor's mansion was occupied by a Democrat, and both houses of the state's legislature were dominated by Democratic members. The pervasive Democratic influence, particularly over the legislative–executive law-making machinery, obviated partisan gridlock that could have encouraged the West Virginia court to fill a policy-making vacuum.

WEST VIRGINIA JUDGES

During the period 1977 through 1986, the backgrounds of the judges of the West Virginia court and the Indiana court during the 1980s were, on balance, similar. During these periods each court had one judge who stood out because of his educational background, his advocacy of judicial activism, and his recognition by others as an agent for change on his court. In West Virginia the outstanding judge was Richard Neely. Before the start of their judicial careers the judges of the West Virginia court had practiced law in somewhat larger communities than their Indiana brethren and their backgrounds were somewhat more cosmopolitan, but the West Virginia bench had written and published fewer articles than their Indiana counterparts so even less is known of their philosophies and beliefs than is known of the Indiana judges. Both courts had a continuing partisan complexion during the period; the West Virginia court was exclusively Democratic and the Indiana Court was predominantly Republican.[35] Except for their prominent members, the composition of either the West Virginia court or the Indiana court, is remarkable.

Justice Neely

Richard Neely was a Democrat and had been selected initially for the court in the judicial election of 1972. Neely had attended Yale University Law School and received his LL.B. degree in 1967. After military service in Viet Nam, he had practiced law in Fairmont, West Virginia, a community of approximately 25,000, and, prior to his election to the court, had served in the state legislature from 1971 to 1973. Early in 1972, Justice Neely had announced his candidacy for nomination for the U.S. Senate in the Democratic primary for the seat held by the popular incumbent, Senator Jennings Randolph, whom he believed would not run for reelection. Neely's grandfather, Mathew M. Neely, had been a popular governor and U.S. Senator from West Virginia and had made the Neely name an enormous electoral asset. The Neely name "ranks next to God in West Virginia,"[36] and, with this asset, the decision of the thirty-year-old political neophyte to seek the U.S. Senate seat was not unreasonable, although possibly premature. He was surprised when Randolph announced that he would run for reelection and quickly switched his candidacy to the race for the West Virginia Supreme Court of Appeals, where his name and Democratic affiliation virtually assured his election against the appointed Republican incumbent.

His education and recognized intelligence qualified him as the intellectual leader of the court. The editor of the Charleston *Gazette* described him as "exceptionally bright and articulate."[37] However, he would not qualify as either a "social or task leader,"[38] roles that Randall Shepard may have assumed on the Indiana court. He was not the recognized leader of the other members of the court as Frank Celebrezze was the acclaimed leader of the majority on the early 1980s Ohio court. The Charleston *Gazette's* editor continued: "He's shot in the ass with himself."[39] The other members of the court are his "fiercest critics" because of this arrogance and his personal publicity seeking.[40] Neely's self-importance created problems even at the level of his relationship with his secretary. He was forced to resign the rotating chief justiceship in 1985 because he was embroiled in a dispute with his secretary over her role as babysitter for his four-year-old son.[41] His idiosyncratic personality is exemplified by his affectation of a cape that cannot fail to get him public notice in rural West Virginia, and his request that a state highway patrol escort walk several paces behind him, presumably to deemphasize his slight, five-foot, six-inch stature.[42]

A West Virginia lawyer and political scientist examined the emergence of activism in the West Virginia court and identified Justice Neely as a "primary catalyst in the Court's transition to a more active role in the public process. (His) style . . . is markedly different from the traditionalistic tone of his predecessors on the court—strong doses of history, sociology, and economics . . . which present arguments from the realm of public policy and political philosophy."[43] Neely's educational background, his intellectual acumen, his published delineation of appropriate judicial activism, and his support for activism as a legitimate judicial role, together with policy rather than "legalistic" support for his decisions, made him the advocate for activism on a court that was more activist than he was.

Justice Neely stood out on the West Virginia court just as Justice Shepard stood out on the Indiana court. Both were graduates of a prestigious national law school. Both had shown an interest in a Washington policy-making role—Shepard had occupied one and Neely had aspired, briefly, to another. Both recognized that judicial activism is a characteristic of a court that is independent of individual preference, partisanship, or ideology. However, there is a significant difference in their approval of activism as a legitimate force in judicial decision making. Shepard's activism was a bulldozer that moved aside the accumulated detritus of traditional judging while Neely's was more like a pair of pruning shears that selected the most promising blooms for activism's vase.

Neely described his understanding of and attachment to judicial activism in an interview that was published in a magazine for trial lawyers.[44] He clarified his belief in the distinctiveness of judicial activism: "Arguments about activism are not the same as . . . about loose v. strict constructionism or conservatism v. liberalism." He had earlier described his approach as "pragmatic or structural, based on the strength and weaknesses as policy makers of the three branches of government. Judicial activism is appropriate in an issue area that does not have enough interest to secure a place on the agenda of the other branches."[45] Courts should intrude "where the bare mechanics of the legislative process frustrates a democratic result." "One good rule of thumb for determining legitimacy of court intrusion into political decision making is to ask: If this issue were brought to the floor of both houses (of the legislature) for a vote, how would it be decided at that stage?"[46] If judicial intervention is "legitimate," the court should make policy if the standards for decision are clear and the means "are within the court's control without placing a heavy administrative burden on the judicial system."[47]

Tort law is an area of the law in which Neely believes the courts are strong and the legislature is weak; it is also an area that lacks sufficient interest to get the attention of the legislature. Regulation of the economy and mental health are other areas that he believes are appropriate for judicial activism. On the other hand, two other questions that were getting much attention by state courts at the time, public school financing and the validity of the death penalty, each generates enough independent public interest to get the attention of the legislature and the executive.[48] Justice Neely dissented when the court invalidated the state's policy for funding for the state's public schools,[49] with "reluctance . . . not because I am less outraged

. . . about the condition of West Virginia schools, but because I am neither Governor nor the entire legislature." He noted that both other branches of state government were actively working on state support for public education "while taking cognizance of other compelling yet competing imperatives" for state resources.[50] Consistently, he dissented when the court struck down the state policy for assessment of real property at 50 percent of its actual value[51] because he believed that the determination of the level of tax assessment is a "political question" that the legislature was competent to settle and then he defended the legislatively established policy, significantly, with policy arguments based on the evils of regressive taxation and the benefits of attracting new industry.

Justice Neely recognized the extremes of the activist-restraintist dimension and carved out a span of judicial activism in the middle, of which he approves. He observed that "(a)ll this is fine in theory where we are dealing with genuine routine, technical issues, but ambitious courts and energetic judges expand the definition of 'routine' and 'technical' to anything which interests them, while modest courts and lethargic judges find security in sedulously following precedent regardless of its wisdom."[52] Like Justice Shepard, Justice Neely has had more of his writings published than is usual for a state court justice.

There has been substantial confusion about Justice Neely's location on the philosophical continuum. In a confusion of political ideology and judicial philosophy, a national commentator has described Neely's early opinions on the court as "some of the Court's most liberal opinions," but concluded that he had become a "voice of judicial restraint."[53] In 1981, he was "viewed as the most conservative member of the West Virginia Supreme Court of Appeals" by a prominent West Virginia lawyer.[54] His descriptions as the most conservative member of the later court and the most liberal member of the earlier court may both be accurate, for they depend on the philosophical position of the court's other members and the 1973–1977 court was substantially more conservative than the court after the judicial election of 1976. In 1985, he described himself as "farther to the right than Jimmy Carter and farther to the left than Ronald Reagan."[55] Regardless, it is clearly incorrect to describe his as a voice of judicial restraint.

Whether a justice is a judicial activist or not depends on whether he/she accepts activism as a legitimate judicial role and the outcome he/she prefers in the pending case. In a particular case, if a justice prefers a decision that is not activist, that justice's decision will appear to be non-activist regardless of whether the justice endorses activism as a legitimate judicial role or not. This non-activist decision might suggest that the justice prefers a restrained judicial role. However, this decision might reflect the justice's philosophical attachment to non-activism or it might be the result of the justice's policy preference. One, or even a number of, non-activist decisions do not support a conclusion that a justice is not an activist. Activism and non-activism are not symmetrical in that respect because one activist decision is evidence that the decision maker accepts activism as a legitimate judicial role; failure to decide any particular case in an activist way is no evidence of preference for the restrained role. Justice Neely's coherent philosophy of activism in judicial decision making resulted in his non-activist decision in cases in which his court's majority was reaching activist results. His activist decision making qualify him as an activist. His non-activist decisions do not disqualify him.

Viewed from this perspective, Neely is a judicial activist. In two tort cases in the year before the post-1976 court was elected, Neely advocated adoption of two novel common-law rules. In one case he was not willing to go as far as the court went, which was the abrogation of the doctrine of parental immunity from suit. However, in his concurring opinion, he advocated a novel policy that would have continued parental immunity as the governing rule except in cases in which the parents had insurance coverage.[56] He valued the policy considerations of family harmony and parental discipline that he believed are promoted by the rule of parental immunity and would have protected them with parental immunity except when liability coverage eliminates a threat to them. In the other case, the court had routinely affirmed the prevailing rule that monetary claims for future medical expenses and for pain and suffering must be supported by proof that they will be incurred.[57] Justice Neely argued persuasively, in dissent, that improvements in probability theory and statistics had removed the fear that an award for future damages would be merely speculative.[58] In both cases his proposal would have changed existing doctrine: in the first the court went further than he would, while in the second, he proposed a change in policy that the court would not accept. However, the court that before Neely's election had been "passive in matters of public policy" was showing the effect of his activist advocacy during the period 1973 to 1976 by reconsidering the state's established common-law doctrines.[59]

In the decade after the court was reconstituted by the 1976 election, the nascent activism that had been aroused by Neely's 1972 election and had begun to express itself in the area of common-law doctrine now came alive, particularly in the court's use of the West Virginia Constitution to make state-level policy.[60] Justice Neely's advocacy of judicial activism prior to 1977 prepared the way for the significantly higher level of policy making after the 1976 judicial election that was nourished by the attitudes of the newly elected justices just as the level of activism in the prior court, although coming alive, was retarded by the attitudes of that court's justices. Justice Neely's votes, consistent in each case with his judicial philosophy, were for the activist decision in nine of the seventeen cases in which he participated and in which there was a potential for an activist result. Significantly, Justice Neely agreed with two revolutionary activist decisions the court made during the period: the adoption of comparative negligence and the relegation of time limitations in workers' compensation cases to procedural, rather than jurisdictional, status. In the latter case Justice Neely wrote the opinion of the court. In all the cases in which he wrote an opinion he supported his decision with policy considerations, unlike the opinions of the other members of the court whose decisions, while frequently more activist in result than his, were supported with tired, traditional legalistic reasoning. Paradoxically, Neely was the catalyst for his court's judicial activism, an activism that was more activist than his judicial philosophy allowed him to be.

Other Members of the Court

The makeup of the West Virginia court after the 1976 judicial elections was the result of three disparate, somewhat conflicting conditions: the traditional predominance of the Democrat party in state politics, a reform movement that had swept over the state in the 1960s and 1970s,[61] and the Republican appointments to the court that had encouraged Democrat candidates to run against the Republican incumbents. Two members of the "new" court were sitting on the court prior to the 1976 election. Fred Caplan was a traditional Democrat who had first been appointed to the court in 1962 and who had served continuously. He had graduated from the University of Richmond Law School in 1941 and after military service in the World War II, had been associated with state government before his accession to the high bench. He had been a member of the West Virginia legislature from 1949 to 1952 and an assistant attorney general from 1953 to 1961. Simultaneously with the first years of his service on the court, he served as a member of the West Virginia Public Service Corporation from 1961 to 1967. He has not written for publication in either professional or academic journals nor has he produced any book-length publication. Richard Neely was the other justice who was sitting before and after the 1976 judicial election.

The judicial election of 1976 added three new members to the court. That election had arrayed two appointed Republican incumbents against two Democratic challengers and a Republican against a Democrat for an "open" seat that had been created by the retirement of a veteran Democratic justice. The three Democratic candidates were successful. Their Democratic labels undoubtedly helped their election prospects, but their liberal political philosophy would have been foreign to many of their party supporters.

West Virginia had become a state because of the rugged individualism of its citizens and their staunch opposition to the secession of Virginia, its mother state, from the Union. But the modern-day border state West Virginians and its Democratic political leaders bear a close resemblance to their Virginia cousins. Their senior U.S. Senator during the period 1977 to 1986 was a former Ku Klux Klan member who voted against civil rights laws during his service in both the U.S. House and Senate.[62] The ordinary West Virginia Democrat tends to be at the conservative end of the ideological spectrum, except in labor matters. "Appalachian's innate resistance to change might always be brought to bear against fundamental changes in the old order."[63] The three new Democratic members of the West Virginia Supreme Court of Appeals did not come from this traditional wing of the party.[64]

These new Democratic justices were relatively young for state high court justices: at the time of their election Justice Darrel McGraw was thirty-eight, Justice Thomas Miller was forty-five and Justice Sam Harshbarger was fifty years old. They were similar in other respects and were, collectively, unremarkable except for their judicial office. Each had graduated from the West Virginia University Law School and none had run for nor been appointed to a governmental office prior to the 1976 election. Neither Justice McGraw nor Justice Harshbarger has any published nonjudicial writing. Justice Miller has published one article. The 1987 volume of the *West Virginia Law Review*, in celebration of its ninetieth anniversary, had invited the court justices to contribute an essay. Justice Miller summarized "The New Federalism in West Virginia," the court's use of state, rather than similar federal, constitutional provisions when it had invalidated West Virginia laws. The essay was a summary of the court's constitutional decisions rather than a prescription for decision making, and gave no indication whether the justice endorsed or deplored the court's use of the West Virginia Constitution to make policy.[65] Two of the new justices would lose their jobs in future Democratic primaries, possibly because of decisions that were driven by their liberal views.[66] There was no suggestion of a potential for judicial activism in their backgrounds. Although each stood out in some contrast to his party, they were an unremarkable collection of high court justices.

WEST VIRGINIA SUPREME COURT OF APPEALS CASES, 1977–1986

A substantial part of the court's activist policy making during the period 1977 to 1986 was in the related areas of tort and workers' compensation. At the beginning of the period the doctrine and rules that prevailed in West Virginia in these two areas were the business-protective doctrine and rules that had been developed in this country during the last half of the nineteenth century when the American courts had been intent on protecting developing American industry. These had made it difficult for an injured person to succeed in the American state courts, including the West Virginia courts. In the interim since their development, most other state courts had modified their doctrine and rules to shift the cost of injuries from the injured individuals to insurance companies and other corporations better able to bear these costs. Prior to the West Virginia judicial election in 1976, the West Virginia court had not changed. The West Virginia court had routinely refused to recognize that new technology and changing conditions had created a need for new causes of action. The result was that plaintiffs in West Virginia either fit their claims into old doctrinal bottles or they went uncompensated. The post-1976 West Virginia court quickly established its role in modifying common-law principles and channeled West Virginia's court-generated body of law into the mainstream of progressive tort and workers' compensation doctrine and rules. The new court did not hesitate to create new causes of action if it discovered a right without a remedy.

Internal governmental controversies provided the court with other opportunities to impose its policy preferences on state government and also to establish its role in governmental policy making. The West Virginia court did not avoid areas where activism would draw it into direct conflict with the other branches of government. Rather, the court seemed to welcome these opportunities. It took up the challenge to discover state authority to assure equal funding for public education in West Virginia after the U.S. Supreme Court had slammed the U.S. Constitution's equal protection door shut on the issue. The late 1970s and the 1980s was a period of recurring turf fights among the three branches of West Virginia government. The West Virginia court did not hesitate to assert the primacy of its rights when the legislature encroached on them, and confidently delimited the powers of the other branches when they collided. These decisions redounded to the ultimate aggrandizement of the court's own power and enhanced the judicial policy-making powers that had engendered them. Although the new West Virginia court seemed very activist to local observers, its activism was neither unbounded nor unanimous. It limited itself in some cases and in some of the cases in which it acted its members were not in a policy-making lockstep.

A Decade of Judicial Policy Making

Unlike the decision making by the Indiana and Ohio courts during comparable periods, the West Virginia court was a policy-making court for a full decade.

The Common Law, Elimination of Restrictive Doctrine. The West Virginia Constitution and the state's law contained commands that seemed to ensure that the common law that was in effect on June 20, 1863, would not be modified by the West Virginia court. Article VIII, Section 13, of the West Virginia Constitution provided:

> Except as otherwise provided in this article, such parts of the common law, and the laws of this State as are in force on the effective date of this article . . . shall be and continue the law of this State until altered or repealed *by the legislature.* (Emphasis added.)

The West Virginia Code, Section 2-1-1, provided.

> The common law of England . . . shall continue in force within the same, except in those respects wherein it was altered by the general assembly of Virginia before the twentieth day of June, eighteen hundred and sixty-three, or has been, or shall be, altered *by the legislature* of this State. (Emphasis added.)

On its face, this language seemed to deprive the West Virginia court of the power to alter or amend common-law rules and doctrines, leaving any change to the state legislature. This restriction was critical to any effort by the West Virginia court to bring the state's tort and workers' compensation law, based substantially in the common law, in line with the modern practice. If the restriction had the effect it seemed to have, the West Virginia court would have been powerless to act. As long as this provision prevented change in the common law rules and doctrine, the court would be impotent. In 1979, the West Virginia court settled any question that it had the power to change the common law of the state that was created by these provisions. It announced that "the courts always had the historic power to evolve and alter the common law which they created."[67] Although the court used this power it had discovered to create new common-law causes of action in tort law, an area in which the court concluded that the court "has traditionally functioned," it did not assume commensurate power in the area of the criminal common law, an area, the court concluded, "in which the legislature has the primary or plenary power."[68] Two dissenting justices disagreed that the legislature and not the court had this power and would have taken the extraordinary step of creating a common-law crime of murder of an unborn child, an exercise of judicial power that only two other state courts had assumed.[69]

With the constitutional barrier out of the way, the court proceeded to modernize the common law rules and doctrines that controlled the West Virginia law of products liability, workers' compensation, and negligence (tort law). In addition to its modernization of existing personal injury doctrine and rules, the court created new common-law causes of action in tort.

Products Liability Doctrinal Change. The post-1976 West Virginia court expeditiously brought the state's common law of products liability[70] in line with that of its more progressive sister states. Traditionally, products liability law required injured parties to prove, as a prerequisite to collection from a manufacturer, that they had a contract with the manufacturer[71] and that some negligence[72] of the manufacturer had caused their injuries. Justice Neely, writing for the court, "found" that the existing, traditional, West Virginia products liability law was "similar" to the progressive, modern, "strict liability in tort."[73] This enabled the West Virginia court to eliminate the hurdles of the traditional law that were difficult for plaintiffs: privity of contract and the negligence of the manufacturer. Its decision required a plaintiff to prove only that some defect in the product caused the injury.[74] The West Virginia court was even more favorable to injured plaintiffs when injuries were caused by dangerous processes, tools, or machines. Justice Neely "found" that West Virginia law makes a manufacturer who engages in a dangerous activity strictly liable to one who is injured by that activity.[75] Although Justice Neely described the court's process as "finding" this progressive doctrine in existing law, the description of the traditional judicial decision-making process—these "finds" —changed the policy of West Virginia with respect to compensation of accident victims and were activist in effect, if not in Neely's description.

Workers' Compensation Doctrinal Change. Workers' compensation was the result of compromise by employers and employees and it was established to enable workers to be compensated for damages related to their employment by an administrative agency rather than a court and without being required to prove that their employer had been negligent. In return the employees gave up the right to use the courts to sue their employers in ordinary civil suits. In West Virginia, the state constitution[76] guaranteed employers this immunity unless an employee's injury resulted from an employer's "specific intent to injure" the employee.[77] The post-1976, West Virginia court made the law more friendly to the injured worker by establishing the less rigorous standard of "willful, wanton, or reckless misconduct" by the employer rather than "specific intent to injure," and by allowing the injured worker-employee to bring an ordinary civil action in intentional injury cases in which the employer's culpability was a question for the jury.[78]

In two of its activist decisions the new West Virginia court moved well beyond the doctrine that had been adopted in even the most progressive states. The schedules that provide time limitations for each step of the workers' compensation process are notorious pitfalls for claimants. In every state, except Arizona, these time limitations were treated as jurisdictional requirements and any deviation from their prescriptions effectively disqualified a claim. The West Virginia court intrepidly walked down the Arizona side of the street. Justice Neely, writing for his court, overruled numerous earlier decisions in an opinion that held that the violation of the prescribed time limits for workers' compensation appeals did not require automatic dismissal of the employee's claim.[79] Prescribed time limits are still important in West Virginia, but as a result of this very progressive decision, a court, in an appropriate case, can accept an employee's excuse for failure to file the application on time.

Judicial Comparative Negligence. The traditional doctrine of contributory negligence defeats an injured party's claim if his/her own negligence has contributed in any way to the injury. The progressive comparative negligence doctrine ameliorates the Draconian effect of contributory negligence and allows a party to be compensated even though his/her negligence may have been partially responsible for the accident. The unanimous West Virginia court took the uncommon step[80] of establishing comparative negligence judicially and declared that fairness favored allowing a party to recover for his injury "so long as his negligence . . . does not equal . . . the negligence . . . of the other parties."[81]

Common Law, New Causes of Action. As appropriate cases presented the court opportunities to "find" new common-law causes of action, it fashioned relief when the new situation required it. Advances in medical science have created circumstances that present courts with claims for damages for "new" injuries; they have created expectations that courts have to address. In West Virginia an additional and unusual new situation was created when the legislature defined a personal right for those with mental illness, but did not provide a concomitant remedy. This right without a remedy demanded that the courts finish the job. The West Virginia court moved with the times and generally, though not always, ordained a cause of action to fill these voids.

Medical science has enabled physicians to maintain some injured persons whom they could not restore to full function in permanent coma-like states. The West Virginia court concluded that it was the policy of tort law in West Virginia to compensate a permanently injured party in such a way as to make him a "whole man" and recognized a new cause of action for "impairment of capacity to enjoy."[82] The general availability of sterilization procedures, the legalization of abortion, and the ability of medical science to predict birth defects created related new medico-legal situations without recognized causes of action. The West Virginia court considered three questions in a single case: the first, whether an action existed for "wrongful pregnancy,"[83] the second, whether the court recognized an action for "wrongful birth,"[84] and the third, whether there was a cause of action for "wrongful life."[85] In this one case the West Virginia court approved the creation of the two new torts of "wrongful pregnancy" and "wrongful birth," but failed to approve an action for "wrongful life."[86]

When the West Virginia legislature defined a right: "no person shall be deprived of any civil right solely by reason of his receipt of services for mental illness,"[87] but provided no remedy for its enforcement, the court used the "implied causes of action" doctrine[88] to create a novel cause of action for a person who had received mental health services against an employer who denied the person employment because of these services.

Sovereign Immunity.[89] The new court took a roller-coaster ride on sovereign immunity, in part propelled by Article VI, Section 35, of the West Virginia Constitution that provided: "The State of West Virginia shall never be made defendant in any court of law or equity." Despite this constitutional provision, the trend of decisions by the West Virginia court had been to chip away at the common law governmental immunity from liability in tort actions.[90] Early in the new court's life, it interrupted the trend toward abrogation and held that constitutional immunity protected a board of education.[91] However, in the next case in which the court had an opportunity, it eliminated the immunity of school boards from suit in tort.[92] A unanimous court concluded in the second case that continuation of the doctrine of sovereign immunity could lead to governmental irresponsibility and that its abolition might have "positive redistributive and allocative effects," a convincing *policy* justification. Most recently, the ride has continued with a remarkable case that unfortunately has not been reported. In that case the court suggested, in dictum, that the state university would be liable for tort damages, but only up to the limits of its liability insurance coverage.[93] This decision suggested that the court was prepared to take the super-activist step of overruling the state constitution's provision that the "state . . . shall never be made defendant" if the state agency had insurance!

Intergovernmental Tensions. The late 1970s and early 1980s were a time of serious economic difficulty for the state as well as its citizens. The unhealthy economy was at least partially responsible for the cases that the court took advantage of to make its most well-known policy assertions. During this period, poor public school districts throughout the country were becoming active in the courts in attempting to ameliorate the difference between their resources and the resources rich districts had. The discrepancy between poor and rich school districts in West Virginia was perhaps aggravated because of the continuing severe economic conditions in the state's poorest areas. The West Virginia court was in the vanguard of state high courts that found independent state constitutional grounds for invalidating a public school finance system after the U.S. Supreme Court had held that the U.S. Constitution did not prohibit this unequal school funding.[94] The West Virginia court concluded that the provisions of West Virginia's Constitution required higher standards of protection than afforded by the U.S. Constitution and that the state constitution required substantially equal funding for all of the state's school districts.[95] Justice Neely dissented, with "reluctance," consistently with his philosophy of judicial policy making.[96] The court continued to make state fiscal policy that favored local school districts by making more tax money immediately available to the local boards of education. Revenue generated by the real property tax is the main support for the West Virginia's public education system. The court invalidated a legislative system of tax assessment that allowed real property to be assessed at only 50 percent of its actual value and ordered that the assessment of all real property in the state should be increased to 100 percent of its value.[97] Justice Neely's philosophy again required him to dissent; he supported the status quo in his dissent, but, significantly, supported the status quo with policy arguments based on the evils of regressive taxation and the benefits that lower assessment rates would have in attracting new industry to West Virginia.

From 1969 to 1977, the government of West Virginia was politically divided: the governor was a Republican and both houses of the legislature were controlled by Democratic majorities. Prior to the judicial election of 1976, the court had been dominated by Republican appointees of the Republican governor[98] and, in any dispute between the Democratic legislature and the governor, it routinely found that the governor had the ultimate power. During this period, power struggles between the governor and the legislature were, not surprisingly, frequently decided in the West Virgnia Court.[99] After the election of 1976, the governorship and both houses of the legislature were controlled by Democrats. Democratic ascendance in both the governor's office and the legislature should have eliminated resort to the court. However, resort to the court to settle state governmental power disputes may have become institutionalized. These power disputes continued to end up in the court, but, with the identity of partisan control of the three branches, the court could no longer make its decisions by reference to partisan politics. Judicial activism achieved the significance that had previously belonged to party. The state's poverty was frequently the immediate cause of the controversies between the governor and the legislature that enabled the court to exercise its policy-making intervention.

The new West Virginia court was not diffident when the legislature threatened the court's prerogatives or when controversies between and among other governmental institutions gave the court an opportunity to establish the state's policy. The court found itself in direct confrontation with the legislature over its annual budget and over its rule that excused graduates of the West Virginia University Law School from taking a bar examination for admission to the practice of law. West Virginia is one of only two states in which the budget request of the judiciary is constitutionally protected.[100] When the legislature decreased five items of the court's judicial budget, the West Virginia court[101] ordered the legislative clerk to replace the court's five original budget requests in their original amounts.[102] Another conflict between the court and the legislature occurred over the "diploma privilege."[103] This contest resulted from both the legislature and the West Virginia court providing for this privilege. Both the court's rules and a statute passed by the legislature excused the graduates of the state law school from passing an examination in order to be admitted to the practice of law. Tension between the legislature and the West Virginia court culminated when the legislature repealed its law. The court's majority saw the legislative repeal as a threat to its exclusive domain of the admission of lawyers to the practice of law and declared that the legislative repeal was invalid because the West Virginia Constitution had vested the court with the sole power to admit lawyers to the practice of law.[104]

The West Virginia court had assertively denied the legislature the power to reduce the amount of the court's requested budget and had moved with alacrity to head off any attempt by the legislature to impinge on its control of admission to the state's bar. It continued to make policy when its own power was not directly threatened, when the controversy was between the other two branches of state government. It took advantage of two power contests between the state legislature and the governor to establish state policy by deciding the immediate cases and, by its decisions, to create future policy-making opportunities. In the first case, the legislature had created a legislative review committee and had given it power to invalidate rules adopted by executive agencies, a general "legislative veto" scheme. The West Virginia court decided that the plan invaded the governor's executive powers.[105] The second case arose from the substantial reduction of the state's tax revenue that was caused by the recession gripping the country in 1981 and aggravated in West Virginia by a coal miner's strike. The legislature had ordered the governor to reduce *all* state spending proportionally, including educational spending. The West Virginia court decided that education enjoyed a "preferred status" and that the governor was not required to make any cuts in the education budget unless they were "factually necessary."[106] These controversies between the governor and the legislature enabled the court to establish its preferred policies of gubernatorial freedom from legislative oversight and from a high budgetary priority for public education. More important for its future role of policy maker, it established itself as the only state institution that could invalidate executive rules and the authoritative arbiter of the "factual necessity" of the state's budget for public education.

Judicial Amendment of Statute. During the 1980s, courts, particularly federal district courts, intervened in the operation of state executive departments and substituted their management decisions for those of state bureaucrats. Prisons, mental hospitals, and school systems were subjected to court management.[107] The West Virginia court did not go so far as to take over the operation of a state institution but, in a remarkable arrogation of the right to amend a legislative act, it added an entirely different class of beneficiaries to the legislature's protection. The legislature had passed a law that authorized the state welfare department to provide protection and services to adults who were mistreated by their caretakers.[108] In response to a petition by "street people," the court found that street people were included in the statute's provision,[109] although the legislature had neither specifically mentioned nor clearly described street people and had apparently intended that the Welfare Department should not provide for them.[110] It is clear that the West Virginia court was anxious to become an important part of the policy-making structure in the state. The disparity between the legislative purpose and intent and the judicial "interpretation" confirms the Charleston *Gazette's* opinion that the court was "trying to mold state government in its own image."

The relationship between activism in the West Virginia court and Richard Neely was less direct than the relationship between the 1985–1990 activism in the Indiana court and Randall Shepard. The Indiana court began to reverse legislative policy almost immediately after Shepard joined the court. The Indiana court that had been a severely restrained decision maker began a period of lively policy making and Shepard was part of the court's majority in each of its activist decisions. There was no precipitate launch into policy making in the West Virginia court following Neely's election in 1972 and during the court's period of high activism, 1977–1986, Neely was not in the court's activist majority in every one of its policy making decisions. The direct and immediate relationship in the Indiana court was not duplicated in West Virginia. Neely's advocacy of judicial policy making had turned the West Virginia court away from traditional decision making and this change and the influence of his continued advocacy of judicial policy making had energized the court to make policy in areas of the law in which Neely believed judicial policy making was not proper.

After the judicial election of 1976, the West Virginia court began a period of vigorous activism; it continued to reexamine and change the court-made common law doctrine; it created new rules when unique circumstances required, and it became the final arbiter of policy disputes between the other branches of West Virginia government. Although Neely had been activism's pioneer on the court when he joined it in 1973, he didn't join the post-1976-election court's activist policy making when its decision making conflicted with his coherent system of proper judicial behavior.

NOTES

1. Michael Barone and Grant Ujifusa, *The Almanac of American Politics 1984* (Washington, D.C.: National Journal, 1983), p. 1253.

2. Michael Barone and Grant Ujifusa, *The Almanac of American Politics 1986* (Washington, D.C.: National Journal, 1985), p. 1430.

3. Barone and Ujifusa, *1984*, p. 1253.

4. Barone and Ujifusa, *1984*, p. 1253.

5. Barone and Ujifusa, *1984*, p. 1254.

6. Barone and Ujifusa, *1986,* p. 1431.

7. Barone and Ujifusa, *1986*, p. 1435.

8. Various Barone and Ujifusa *Almanacs* from 1968.

9. John P. Hagan, "Policy Activism in the West Virginia Supreme Court of Appeals, 1935–1985," *West Virginia Law Review* 89 (1986): 149–165.

10. Bradley C. Canon and Lawrence Baum, "Patterns of Adoption of Tort Law Innovation: An Application of Diffusion Theory to Judicial Doctrines," *American Political Science Review* 75 (1981): 975–987.

11. Gregory Caldeira, "On the Reputation of State Courts," *Political*

Behavior 5 (1983): 83.

12. Hagan, "Policy Activism," p. 149.

13. Hagan, "Policy Activism," p. 150.

14. Caldeira, "On the Reputation"; Canon and Baum, "Patterns of Adoption"; Hagan, "Policy Activism" and Ode, "West Virginia Justice."

15. *Lancaster v. The Potomac Edison Company of West Virginia*, 192 S.E.2d 234 (1972).

16. *Peneschi v. National Steel Corp.*, 295 S.E.2d 1 (1982). "Strict liability" is the progressive doctrine, "negligence" is the traditional doctrine.

17. *Jones, et al. v. Laird Foundation, Inc., et al.*, 195 S.E.2d 821 (1973); *Spaulding v. State Workmen's Compensation Commission, et al.*, 205 S.E.2d 130 (1974); *Sizemore v. Workmen's Compensation Commission, et al.*, 219 S.E.2d 912 (1975).

18. *Lee v. Comer and Lee*, 224 S.E.2d 721 (1976)—abrogation of parental immunity; *Ohio Valley Contractors v. Board of Education, et al.*, 293 S.E.2d 437 (1982)—sovereign immunity; *Bradley v. Appalachian Power Company*, 256 S.E.2d 879 (1979)—comparative negligence.

19. *Grob v. Reece*, 214 S.E.2d 330 (1975); *Louk v. Haynes*, 223 S.E.2d 780 (1976).

20. *Brotherton v. Blankenship*, 207 S.E.2d 421 (1973); *Brotherton v. Blankenship*, 214 S.E.2d 467 (1975) and *Joint Committee etc. et al. v. Bonar*, 230 S.E.2d 629 (1976).

21. See, Table 3.1, A-Precedent.

22. One of the vacancies was created by the resignation of Justice Sprouse who resigned to accept appointment to the federal bench.

23. Hagan, "Policy Activism," p. 152.

24. John H. Rogers, review of *How the Courts Govern America* in *West Virginia Law Review* 81 (1981): 1–44.

25. Hagan, "Policy Activism," p. 152.

26. Hagan, "Policy Activism," p. 152.

27. Charleston, West Virginia, *Gazette*, January 1, 1984, p. 1B.

28. Norman Ode, "West Virginia Justice Loses Bitter Primary Race," *The National Law Journal*, 10 (May 30,1988): 3, at p. 10.

29. Hagan measured the level of judicial activism as the percentage that "activist" decisions were of a random selection of 10 percent of the cases decided by the court. His activist cases were (1) those in which the court decided against a non-judicial government party, and (2) those in which the court expressly overruled, disapproved, or discarded its own precedent. His level of activism was calculated according to a weighting formula that gave a value of one to a case that was decided against a governmental actor and a two to a ruling disregarding precedent. He had earlier determined the activism levels of other state high courts, presumably by the same measure, and concluded that the level of activism of the West Virginia court from 1977 to 1985 was comparable to the activism of the California, New Jersey, and Michigan courts during their activist periods. Hagan, "Policy Activism."

30. Charleston, West Virginia, *Gazette*, January 1, 1984, p. 1B.

31. West Virginia Constitution, Article 8, Section 4.

32. The 1976 information is from *State Caseload Statistics: Annual Report 1976* (Williamsburg, Va.: National Center for State Courts, 1977) at p. 377. The 1986 information is from *State Caseload Statistics: Annual Report 1986* (Williamsburg, Va.: National Center for State Courts, 1987) at p. 150.

33. West Virginia Constitution, Article VIII, Section 2.

34. West Virginia Constitution, Article VIII, Section 2.

35. The West Virginia justices' biographic information is found in various editions of *The American Bench, Judges of the Nation* (Minneapolis: Reginald Bishop, Forster & Associates).

36. Darcy Frey, "Jurist Provocateur," *American Lawyer* 7 (June, 1985): 105–107.

37. Frey, "Jurist Provocateur," p. 106.

38. David J. Danelski, "Values as Variables in Judicial Decision Making: Notes Toward a Theory," *Vanderbilt Law Review* 19 (1966): 721–740.

39. Frey, "Jurist Provocateur," p. 106.

40. Frey, "Jurist Provocateur," p. 107.

41. Patty Vandegrift, "State Panel Probes West Virginia Justices Use of Staff," *The National Law Journal* 7 (July 15, 1985): 6.

42. Vandegrift, "State Panel," p. 6.

43. John P. Hagan, "Policy Activism in the West Virginia Supreme Court of Appeals, 1935–1985," *West Virginia Law Review* 89 (1986): 149–165.

44. The Hon. Richard K. Neely, "A Structural View of Judicial Activism," *Trial* 20 (No. 4, April, 1984): 79.

45. The Hon. Richard K. Neely, *How Courts Govern America* (New Haven: Yale University Press, 1981).

46. Neely, *How Courts*, p. 73.

47. Neely, *How Courts*, pp. 145–146.

48. Neely, *How Courts*, pp. 16, 170–189.

49. *Pauley v. Kelly*, 255 S.E.2d 859 (1979).

50. *Pauley v. Kelly*. Neely later distinguished the school finance case from areas of the law in which it is appropriate for a court to intervene: "in the area of schools there is no political indifference. . . . While in all the other areas, the legislative process was characterized by inertia, in the school cases it us characterized by frenetic activity." Neely, *How Courts*, p. 177. It may be of interest that Justice Neely reportedly entered his son in Eton shortly after his birth. Frey, "Jurist Provocateur," p. 106.

51. *Boggs v. Board of Education, et al.*, 244 S.E.2d 799 (1978).

52. Neely, *How Courts*, p. 43.

53. Frey, "Jurist Provocateur," pp. 105, 107.

54. John H. Rogers, review of *How Courts Govern America* in *West Virginia Law Review* 81 (1981): 1–44.

55. Frey, "Jurist Provocateur," p. 106.

56. *Lee v. Comer*, 224 S.E.2d 721 (1976).

57. *Ellard v. Henry*, 231 S.E.2d 339 (1976).

58. Justice Neely had proposed the new rule in an earlier case, *Jordan v. Bero*, 210 S.E.2d 618 (1974) at p. 640. He noted, in his concurring opinion in *Ellard* that his proposal had been "enthusiastically endorsed" in a law review article by Leonard Grumbach, "Awarding Damages for Permanent Injuries: A Proposal to Eliminate the Unreasonableness of 'Reasonable Certainty' in *Jordan v. Bero,*" *Hofstra Law Review* 4 (1976): 101–114.

59. See Table 3.1.

60. See Table 3.1.

61. Neal R. Pierce, *The Border States: People, Politics and Power in Five Border South States* (New York: Norton, 1975); John P. Hagan, "Policy Activism in the West Virginia Supreme Court of Appeals, 1935–1985," *West Virginia Law Review* 89 (1986):149–165.

62. Barone and Ujifusa, *1986.*

63. Pierce, *The Border States*, p. 34.

64. Hagan, "Policy Activism," p. 152.

65. The Hon. Thomas Miller, "The New Federalism in West Virginia," *West Virginia Law Review* 89 (1987): 212.

66. Norman Ode, "West Virginia Justice Loses Bitter Primary Race," *The National Law Journal* 10 (May 30, 1988): 3, 10.

67. *Morningstar v. Black and Decker Manufacturing Co.*, 253 S.E2d 666 (1979).

68. *State, ex rel. Atkinson v. Wilson*, 332 S.E.2d 807 (1984), 810.

69. See *State v. Horne*, 310 S.E.2d 703 (1984), South Carolina and *Commonwealth v. Cass, 467 N.E.2d 1324 (1984),* Massachusetts.

70. Products liability law is that area of the law that considers the liability of the manufacturer of a product to compensate one who is injured by a product that is defective.

71. The doctrine of "privity of contract."

72. Negligence is a concept of personal injury (tort) law that allows an injured party to be compensated by the party (defendant) causing the injury only if the defendant failed to exercise the care an ordinary person would exercise in the circumstance.

73. Strict liability in tort is a doctrine that relieves an injured person of the requirement to prove that he/she had a contract with the defendant and of the duty to prove that the injury was caused by the defendant's negligence.

74. *Morningstar*, p. 680.

75. *Peneschi v. National Steel Corp.*, 295 S.E.2d 1 (1982).

76. West Virginia Constitution, Article 4, Section 2.

77. *Allen v. Raleigh-Wyoming Mining Co.*, 186 S.E. 612 (1939).

78. This decision not only lowered the requirements for maintaining a cause of action, it gave the injured employee a plaintiff-friendly institution, the jury, to apply it. Jury awards are substantially higher than the awards of administrative

agencies for similar injuries. The agencies are generally limited by a rigid schedule of permissible awards for described injuries.

79. *Bailey v. State Workmen's Compensation Commissioners*, 296 S.E.2d 901 (1982)

80. In a negligence-based system of compensation the plaintiff either gets the total amount of the jury's evaluation of the injury or nothing. There is no conceptual continuum that spans the middle ground. This makes it very difficult for courts, whose stock-in-trade is concepts, to move from contributory to comparative negligence and is the reason that only four states had replaced contributory with comparative negligence *by judicial* decision before the West Virginia court adopted it. See Martin Shapiro, "Decentralized Decision Making in the Law of Torts," *Political Decision Making*, S. Sidney Ulmer, ed. (New York: Van Nostrand, 1970).

81. *Bradley v. Appalachian Power Company*, 256 S.E.2d 879 (1979).

82. *Bradley*, p. 675.

83. An action by the parents for a subsequent birth of a child against a physician who had performed a sterilization procedure on one of the parents.

84. An action by the parents of a child who had been born with a birth defect against a physician who had failed to give them genetic information that was necessary for them to make an informed choice whether to begin or continue an existing pregnancy.

85. An action by a child who has been born with a birth defect against a physician who failed to give its parents genetic information necessary for them to make an informed choice whether or not to have an abortion.

86. *James G. v. Caserta*, 332 S.E.2d 872 (1985). Although the court's decision creating two new causes of action was intentional judicial policy making, it did not ground its decision in policy consideration. In concluding that parents had a cause of action for "wrongful birth" while the defective child did not have a cause of action for "wrongful life" in the same situation, the court relied on legalistic reasoning based on "rights"and "duties" and failed to address the policy questions such as who should have the financial responsibility for the correction of the defect and for support of the defective child.

87. West Virginia Code, 27-5-9(a).

88. A doctrine that allows courts to create civil remedies for violations of statutes for which the legislature has provided no relief. See John H. Bauman, "Implied Causes of Action in the State Courts," *Stanford Law Review* 30(1978):1243.

89. A doctrine that provides that a governmental institution, a nation, state, or subdivision, cannot be sued without its consent.

90. See "Survey of Developments," *West Virginia Law Review* 81 (1978): 279–454, 340, note 358.

91. *Boggs v. Board of Education, et al.*, 244 S.E.2d 799 (1978). Consistently, the court's analysis was grounded in legalistic reasoning that depended on the source of the Board's funds and the kind of function it performed, rather than policy concerns such as relative ability of the Board and the injured

child-plaintiff to bear the loss and the effect of its decision on the encouragement of safety.

92. *Ohio Valley Contractors v. Board of Education, et al.*, 293 S.E.2d 437 (1982).

93. *Pittsburgh Elevator Company v. Board of Regents*, No. 15438 (June 30, 1983) unreported.

94. See *San Antonio School District v. Rodriguez*, 411 U.S. 1 (1973).

95. *Pauley v. Kelly*, 255 S.E.2d 859 (1979).

96. Justice Neely explained that the school finance case was not suitable for judicial policy making because (1) the management of the schools is the result of political compromise and judicial interference with one aspect would cause disruption to others thought to be settled, (2) the relief sought was the provision of money that Neely feels is the particular prerogative of the legislature and if a court appropriates money for one educational purpose it loses its "neutrality" and incurs the hostility of all other vested interests, (3) the judicial enforcement of the constitutional standard, "thorough and efficient," would have required the court to become involved in the active management of the schools, an area in which "courts have absolutely no expertise" and for which, he believes, they are "remarkably unsuited," (4) there is no agreement in society or in the courts as to what appropriate reform should be, both the means and the ends "are up for grabs." Neely, *How Courts,* pp. 188–89.

97. *Killen v. Logan County Commissioners*, 295 S.E. 2d 689 (1982). This decision increased the revenue of some school districts up to 100 percent of their previous revenue.

98. Hagan, "Policy Activism."

99. See *Brotherton v. Blankenship*, 207 S.E.2d 421 (1973); *Brotherton v. Blankenship*, 214 S.E.2d 467 (1975) and *Joint Committee etc. et al. v. Bonar,* 230 S.E.2d 629 (1976).

100. The other is Wisconsin. See West Virginia Constitution, Article 6, Section 51, subsection B(5).

101. Four of the five members of the court had recused themselves; only Justice McGraw was on the special panel that the court appointed to hear the case.

102. *State, ex rel. Bagley v. Blankenship*, 246 S.E.2d 99 (1978).

103. The privilege that graduates of the West Virginia University Law School have to be excused from the requirement that they pass an examination in order to be admitted to the practice of law in West Virginia is known locally as the "diploma privilege."

104. *State ex rel. Quelch v. Daugherty*, 306 S.E.2d 233 (1983). The court's decision made the clear policy that it alone controlled admission to the practice of law in West Virginia and the legislature was not to interfere but its analysis of the question and support for its decision were pedestrian. Justice Neely's concurring opinion offered policy support for the "diploma privilege": "I despise bureaucratic requirements that demand that people perform vain acts. In a state like West Virginia where we have a competent law school specializing in West Virginia

Law, a bar examination becomes nothing but a nuisance." *Quelch v. Daugherty*, pp. 236–7.

105. *State ex rel. Barker v. Mandhin, et al.*, 279 S.E.2d 622 (1981).

106. *State ex rel. Board of Education v. Rockefeller*, 281 S.E.2d 131 (1981).

107. See The Hon. Frank M. Johnson, "The Constitution and the Federal Judge," in *Perspectives on American Government*, William Lasser, ed. (Lexington, Mass.: Heath, 1992).

108. "persons who by reason of physical, mental or other infirmity are unable to independently carry on the daily activities . . . necessary to sustaining life and reasonable health" West Virginia Code, Sec. 9-6-1. See "Survey of Developments in West Virginia Law," *West Virginia Law Review* 86 (1984) 480–685, p. 485, note 44.

109. *Hodge v. Ginsberg*, 303 S.E.2d 245 (1983).

110. "Survey of Developments in West Virginia Law," *West Virginia Law Review* 86 (1984): 480–685.

Chapter 4

Ohio

Ohio is generally considered a midwestern state although it is the extreme eastern anchor of the Midwest and its industrial northeastern and eastern regions are closely associated with its neighboring eastern states, New York and Pennsylvania, while much of southern Ohio is closely related culturally with its border state neighbors across the Ohio River, West Virginia and Kentucky. The economy of Ohio is moderately varied and variably stable: basic manufacturing in the northeast and east, smaller and more diversified manufacturers and service producers in its center and in the Cincinnati area, and agriculture in the rural center and south provide a mix that insulates it from wild statewide economic swings. The original Ohio settlers came to northeastern Ohio from New England and to southern Ohio from Virginia,[1] creating a state culture divided by Interstate 70 across the center of the state. The northwest farm lands were claimed by German immigrants; Eastern and Southern European immigrants came to eastern Ohio to work in the coal mines and steel mills and crowded the established Yankees to work in the steel mills in the Cleveland area.

Ohio was the first state created from the Northwest Territory and the "first entirely American state."[2] The concern and provision for public support for education in the Northwest Ordinance and its prohibition of slavery enabled Ohio to become a "liberal republic" with free labor and "one of the most productive parts of western civilization,"[3] the home of steel, soap, tool, tire, rubber, and glass manufacturers.

Ohio has been a closely divided state politically. The Democrat and Republican parties have shared Ohio governor's office and the state legislature. From the end of the Civil War until the Great Depression, the Republican Party was dominant. During this period Ohio sent six of the nation's seven presidents to Washington, all of whom were Republicans. Since the Depression, the parties have alternated control of the branches of state government as well as Ohio's U.S. Senate seats, often with one party's total dominance followed by total control by the other. Ohio's closely competitive political system that frequently reflects the result in presidential elections[4] and its varied economy seem to be the "epitome of American normalcy."[5] Republican judges have predominated in statewide judicial elections. Over its history, the parties have shared control of the Ohio court, with Republicans having the historic edge.

THE OHIO SUPREME COURT

Judicial Mediocrity

The justices of the Ohio Supreme Court have been nominated in partisan primaries and elected in nonpartisan general elections for most of this century. Ohio is the only state to employ this hybrid selection system, which was the product of the success of the efforts of the progressive movement of the early twentieth century to eliminate partisan politics from government.[6] Paradoxically, the attempt to remove the influence of partisan politics from judicial selection resulted in a strongly partisan judicial selection system, albeit uni-partisan, not bi-partisan. Repeated attempts by the Ohio Bar Association to have a merit system adopted for the selection of Ohio judges have failed.[7]

Prior to 1978, the membership of the Ohio court bench, whether initially selected by gubernatorial appointment or in nonpartisan general elections, had been "overwhelmingly Republican."[8] Republican judicial candidates regularly won statewide judicial elections in Ohio and Democrats regularly lost. This pattern was true for judges who were initially appointed as well as those initially elected. Republicans who had been initially appointed to the high court had usually been elected in the next judicial election while appointed Democrats had regularly failed to retain their seats.[9]

During the first three-quarters of this century, the Ohio court did not make waves on the doctrinal seas and its sister courts largely ignored its decisions. It was satisfied to sail along unnoticed and unremarked in the wake of its more progressive counterpart courts. Although in 1885 West Publishing Company had included the Ohio court in its prestigious Northeast region,[10] by 1910 its reputation was only tenth among state high courts;[11] by 1920 it had slipped to twenty-third and had moved only to twenty-first in 1975.[12] Similarly, the Ohio court neither developed nor was quick to adopt new tort doctrine but was satisfied to follow along and accommodate the "new law" once other courts had defined it and demonstrated its usefulness. The Ohio court ranked thirteenth in the alacrity with which it introduced new tort doctrine prior to World War II and eighteenth in the postwar period.[13]

These separate rankings of the court's reputation and innovation confirm that the pre-1978 Ohio court's orientation reflected the traditional jurisprudence and that "(i)ssues on the cutting edge of social change have tended to evoke a negative response."[14] Unlike the Indiana court, the Ohio court did not have a prolonged deterioration, and unlike the West Virginia court, it did not bring up the rear. It moved steadily along in the middle. It did not have the characteristics of either a strongly activist or a decidedly non-activist appellate court.

The results of Ohio Supreme Court elections since the birth of the Republican Party, roughly the time of the Civil War until 1978, reveal that a substantial preponderance of successful candidates had been nominated in Republican Party conventions or in Republican primaries.[15] Because of the regular success of Republican judicial candidates, the pre-1978 Ohio court was "dominated" by "old stock Republicans."[16] It was a conservative court that shared its values with "small town and rural Ohioans, with business and industry" and it did not disturb legislative policy.[17] The exceptional Democratic justice who sat on the court was either there as a result of appointment by a Democratic governor and was doomed to be defeated at the next election,[18] or was philosophically indistinguishable from the majority Republicans and was willing to be mistaken for one in the nonpartisan general election.[19] This nondescript, conservative court changed radically as a result of the 1978 judicial election, a change that was to augur a short period of unique and intense activity.

The long-running Republican control of the court had been broken briefly during the period 1960 to 1962. This Democratic court "did little to distinguish itself" from traditional Republican courts and lasted only until the next judicial election in 1962.[20] After the 1970 judicial elections, the Republicans had claimed all seven seats, before the Republican dominance gradually declined during the 1970s. The Democrats again gained a majority, four–three, after the 1978 election. This majority was to increase to five–two after the 1980 election and six–one after the 1982 election. A casual examination of the general elections in the late 1970s yields no explanation of the reversal of Republican fortunes. It is unlikely that it was related to statewide nonjudicial partisan politics. Former Republican Governor James A. Rhodes had broken a four-year Democratic hold on all statewide offices by recapturing the governor's office in the 1974 election and he was reelected four years later.

It is more likely that during this period the Republican judicial candidates were on the wrong side of the incumbency and familiar name advantages. Although incumbency has less advantage in judicial than legislative and executive races because of general inattention of the voter to the personnel of the courts, it does help in fund raising, and money was a factor that was assuming a greater importance in Ohio High Court races at the end of the 1970s. Incumbency does add to a candidate's name familiarity, which is always important in relatively low information judicial contests.[21] The most likely nemesis of the Republican candidates in these years was the familiarity the judicial voter had with the Democrats' surnames, Sweeney, Celebrezze, and Brown.[22] In the name game, Republican candidates Marcus, Dowd, Harper, Krupansky, and McCormac were mismatched against Democrats Sweeney, Celebrezze, and, particularly Brown, whom the persistent Republican judicial voter could easily have confused with one of "their" Browns.

Sudden Activism

The change in the court shaped by the 1978 election was abrupt. Overnight the quiet, conservative, rural Ohio and business-oriented court became "pro-labor and highly urban."[23] This switch was manifested in policy-making activity in the six-year period from 1981 through 1986 that exceeded in volume that of the comparable period of judicial activism in Indiana in the late 1980s and the longer period of activism in West Virginia. From 1981 through 1986, the Ohio court abrogated four common-law tort immunity doctrines, eliminated three significant limitations on workers' compensation awards, judicially recognized comparative negligence, and either overruled precedent or struck down legislative acts to "shake-up" the somnolent Ohio jurisprudence.

This frenetic activity, though greater in volume, was neither as broad nor as opportunistic as the similar behavior of the Indiana or West Virginia courts. Ohio activist decisions during the period 1981 to 1986 predominantly benefited the economic underdog at the expense of his upperdog counterpart and facilitated the redistribution of society's economic assets. The Indiana and West Virginia courts made activist decisions with redistributive effects, but in these states activism had also flowered in other areas of the law unrelated to class based economics. The Indiana court's activist decisions had also modified the Indiana criminal and commercial law; the West Virginia court's activism reordered school finance and the power relations of the state government. Unlike these courts, the Ohio court's activist decisions were limited to cases in which its decision would directly benefit the working class. The Ohio court ignored its opportunities to equalize statewide school financing, to implement the attractive nuisance doctrine,[24] and to recognize new common-law criminal defenses. The court's eagerness to discard outmoded precedent, to embrace new doctrines, and to innovate in economic cases, was not matched "by a similar enthusiasm in . . . civil rights and liberties cases." The Democratic Court's decisions in non-economic cases were "in keeping with the spirit of deferential Republican courts."[25]

This brief, though intense, period of judicial activism was terminated by the 1986 judicial election that eliminated the short-lived Democratic majority and retired Chief Justice Frank Celebrezze. The successor court, during the period 1987 to 1991, retreated from the frontiers of sovereign immunity and workers' compensation carved out by the Celebrezze court and refused an opportunity to recognize a new redistributive common-law cause of action. However, its retreat was from the Celebrezze court's outposts but not to the settled backwater of traditional Republican courts. In its retreat this Republican-dominated court was not as active as its predecessor, yet its activism was more varied; it did make activist decisions that benefited the working "underdog," but it also recognized a progressive new and controversial criminal defense that its predecessor had rejected.

There were no structural changes in the Ohio court or the Ohio court system during the period 1981 to 1991. The court had seven justices who were elected for six-year terms[26] in nonpartisan general elections after they had been nominated in partisan primaries. The system had an intermediate appellate court that reduced the Ohio court's caseload by filtering out the routine cases and allowed it considerable discretion over its docket.[27] The filter of an intermediate appellate court and discretion over its docket gave the court freedom to use its available time to consider the kinds of cases it wanted to decide. This control of the court's docket created a caseload in 1986 of ninety-one pending cases for each justice that compares favorably with the caseloads of the West Virginia and Indiana caseloads of ninety-nine and one hundred forty-three, respectively, for the same year.[28] Unlike either the Indiana court or the West Virginia court, the chief justiceship of the Ohio court was a separate and distinct seat on the court.[29] It was filled in a regularly recurring judicial election. The judicial elections that were held in 1980 and 1986 for the full six-year term beginning January 1 of the succeeding year were for the chief justice seat and were won by Frank Celebrezze and Thomas Moyer, respectively.

The structure of the Ohio judicial system with its intermediate appellate courts and separate elections for its chief justice was unchanged from prior to the adoption of Ohio's Modern Courts Amendment in 1964 and was the same during the court's traditionalist, pre-1978 election period, during the frenetic 1981 to 1986 period, and the following period of reduced but significant activism.

OHIO JUDGES

The backgrounds of the members of the Ohio court from 1981 to 1991 were substantially different from those of the members of the Indiana and West Virginia courts. The educational and professional lives of the Ohio justices were more cosmopolitan than their counterparts to the west and east.[30] More than a third of the Ohio court judges who served during the decade had received their legal education at a national law school.[31] All except one had practiced law in a metropolitan area with a population in excess of 500,000 people.[32] This was consistent with the Ohio practice of selecting its supreme court judges from its large cities. Twelve of the fourteen justices were initially selected in competitive elections, which is similar to West Virginia where all had been initially elected, but unlike Indiana where only two of the seven justices had been initially elected.

In keeping with the partisan political reputation of the Ohio court, the judges had played varied political roles prior to their ascent to the bench. Two had been candidates for governor of Ohio[33] and two had served as the highest policy adviser to Ohio governors.[34] One had been appointed and served as Ohio's attorney general[35] while one had been the mayor of Ohio's largest city and another had been a candidate for the post.[36] Two of the judges had served in the state legislature prior to their service on the court and one had occupied a leadership position.[37] One had been a resident of Hawaii prior to its statehood and had been appointed Territorial Treasurer by President Truman.[38] One of the high court members had been a city councilman prior to his election to the court and has been mentioned as a possible candidate for mayor of his hometown while sitting on the court.[39] All except two had participated in a partisan election prior to their initial runs for their high court seats.[40]

None of these judges of the Ohio court has published an explanation of his or her preferred judicial role comparable to the elucidating articles and books that Shepard and Neely have written. As a matter of fact, these well-educated justices have written very little. Their remarks when sworn in as a member of the court, when welcoming a group of lawyers newly admitted to the bar, and when addressing an important professional meeting were usually recorded in a bar association publication but they are the earnest but bland description of the court and its workings that are generally expected on these occasions.

Justice Frank Celebrezze

As in the Indiana and West Virginia courts, there was one member of the Ohio court who stood out, Frank Celebrezze, but in Ohio his prominence resulted from his political ambition and not because of his education or his indorsement of judicial activism. Celebrezze's interest in judicial activism was only in its service to his political goals. He was interested in the effect that judicial policy making could have on his chosen political constituency.

Frank Celebrezze was born and lived in Cleveland, Ohio, and was educated in a law school in his home town. He was elected to the chief justice seat on the Ohio Supreme Court in 1978, but his position of power on the court resulted from his leadership of the court's Democratic majority from 1979 to 1987 and not his formal position. His statewide electoral history and success during the 1970s made him a natural leader of the other Democratic judges as they joined him on the court. He was the first Democrat elected to the Ohio court at a time when all the other judges were Republicans and he was the vanguard of the Democratic judges who were to become the court's majority during its period of high activism in the first half of the 1980s.

The status that he gained by being the Democrat groundbreaker on the Ohio court was enhanced among the other Democratic justices by his greater electoral experience and successes. As a result of Ohio's election laws, he had been required to run in, and had won, four statewide elections between 1972 and 1981. His elevation to the court resulted from his victory over an appointed Republican incumbent in a 1972 judicial race to fill the remaining two years of an unexpired term.[41] He joined a court on which the other six justices were Republican. He was not to be joined by a Democrat for four years, during which time he won a judicial election in 1974 for the full six-year term. It was not until 1977 that Democrats Sweeney and Locher joined him. In the election in 1978, he defeated Justice Thomas Herbert, who had, perhaps, the most popular Ohio Republican electoral name of the era.[42] The electoral history of Frank Celebrezze and the other members of the Ohio Supreme Court during the period 1981 to 1991 is contained in Table 4.1.

Table 4.1
Electoral History of the Justices Who Sat on the Ohio Supreme Court, 1981–1991

YEAR	SEAT #1 (CJ)	SEAT #2	SEAT #3	SEAT #4	SEAT #5	SEAT #6	SEAT #7
1988 (election)						Sweeney (D)	Resnick (D)
1986 (election)	Moyer (R)	Holmes (R)	H..Brown (D)				
1984 (election)				Douglas (R)	Wright (R)		
1982 (election)					J. Celebrezze (D)	Sweeney (D)	Locher (D)
1981					Krupansky[1] (R)		
1980 (election)	F. Celebrezze (D)	Holmes (R)	C. Brown (D)				
1979		Holmes[2] (R)					
1978 (election)	F. Celebrezze[3] (D)			W. Brown (D)	P. Brown (R)		
1976 (election)						Sweeney (D)	Locher (D)
1974 (election)		F. Celebrezze (D)					
1972 (election)		F. Celebrezze[4] (D)			P.Brown (R)		

[1] Appointed by Republican Governor James A. Rhodes to fill vacancy created by the resignation of Justice Paul Brown.
[2] Appointed by Republican Governor James A. Rhodes to fill vacancy created by the resignation of Justice Frank Celebrezze upon his election as chief justice.
[3] Associate Justice F. Celebrezze ran to fill the unexpired term in the chief justice seat created by the death of Chief Justice William O'Neill.
[4] Election to fill the unexpired term created by the death of Justice Mathias.

Unlike Justices Shepard and Neely, it is not possible to glean Chief Justice Celebrezze's preferred judicial role from either his judicial or extra-judicial writings. His writing does not reveal a description of his preferred judicial role, but it leaves no doubt that he believed that the Ohio court's decisions should be used to advance the interests of Ohio workers. Chief Justice Celebrezze repeatedly voted to reverse both legislatively and judicially established policies that adversely affected the working Ohioan; consequently, he was clearly an activist, and his commentary leaves no doubt that his activism was intentional. However, his judicial activism was not across-the-board. It was limited and selective: he voted to invalidate legislation and to overrule precedent when it would appeal to Ohio's blue-collar Democrats but he would not upset the status quo in social issue cases when to do so would offend this same group. The Ohio Democratic voter, particularly the blue-collar worker, is not a social liberal. "The candidate who . . . was in favor of the full lunch pail and capital punishment and was opposed to higher taxes, gambling, prostitution, and other forms of organized crime" attracted the votes of the low income, Ohio voter.[43] Frank Celebrezze's judicial decision making was consistent with the political profile of Ohio's blue-collar Democrat. His ambition to be the Democratic candidate for governor of Ohio drove his preference for activist decisions that benefited the working men and women of Ohio economically. It also caused him to prefer status quo, non-activist decisions that protected middle-class social values.

The period of Frank Celebrezze's chief justiceship was an unusually political period for a "nonpartisan" court. Chief Justice Celebrezze used the Ohio court as an adjunct to his political machine. In 1982, he cancelled a contract that the Ohio court had had for fifty years with the Ohio Bar Association for the initial publication of the court's decisions because the Bar Association had investigated his nonjudicial political activity[44] and because the Bar Association had evaluated his younger brother, James, "unqualified" as a candidate that year for an associate justice seat on the Ohio court.[45] Two years later, in 1984, James Celebrezze was again a candidate for the court, this time for a full term. The court had decided that Ohio utility companies owed their customers a refund.[46] Celebrezze arranged that these refunds would be paid by supreme court checks over his signature, which would be mailed shortly before the election in which his brother was a candidate.[47] While chief justice, Frank Celebrezze acted as if he were a candidate for gubernatorial nomination, in apparent violation of the court's Canon 7 (A)(3). He regularly spoke at Democratic political fundraisers, although he had not announced a candidacy for any office; he allowed as many as three groups to raise campaign money for him personally and he heard and decided cases in which his political supporters were involved or interested.[48]

Frank Celebrezze maneuvered for the Democratic nomination for governor of Ohio twice after 1972, the year he joined the Ohio court. In early 1978, the year of his successful race for chief justice, he had unsuccessfully sought the state Democratic organization's screening committee endorsement for a race in the Democratic primary for governor. He turned to the race for chief justice only after that endorsement was denied.[49] In an incredible political farce in 1982, he resigned from the court and announced his candidacy for governor on one day, only to change his mind the next when he revoked his resignation and resumed his official and effective leadership of the court.[50] That year the Democratic nomination for governor went to Richard Celeste who was subsequently elected in the general election and, as the incumbent, was virtually certain to be renominated in 1986. Celebrezze's indecision in 1982 eliminated what would have been his last realistic opportunity to be the Democratic candidate for governor. The Celeste victory in 1982, coupled with his own defeat in 1986, eliminated him as a viable gubernatorial candidate. However, the chief justice could not have known that his ambition was doomed as he and the court approached the high-water mark of the court's activism. His last defeat was still in the future in 1984 when the campaign manager of his aborted 1982 venture for the governorship offered an evaluation of the Celebrezze ambition: "(O)ne cannot discount his dream of being governor of this state for the last quarter century."[51]

Frank Celebrezze described the Ohio court during his chief justiceship as the "peoples court." He first applied the phrase to the court in an article introducing the *Ohio Northern University Law Review* summary of the court's decisions of the 1983–84 term.[52] This name reflected the chief's populist bent[53] and his belief that the court's decisions should serve populist goals.[54] In an earlier introductory article in the same law review, he had explained that the court's judicial activism, "its willingness to depart from precedent," reflected its "progressive attitude" toward protection of the individual.[55] In his concurring opinion in the court's landmark decision that allowed an injured worker to avoid the limitations of the workers' compensation system and to maintain a civil suit against an employer for an intentional tort, the chief branded the dissenters as "anti-worker" in contrast to his and the court's pro-worker stance.[56]

Frank Celebrezze was regularly and generously supported in his judicial races by organized labor[57] and the Celebrezze-led court's class-based decision making fairly repaid their support. The political philosophy that guided his decisions in economic cases was joined in his political personality with a demanding moral posture. He sounded suspiciously like the "religious right" when he blamed "counterculture philosophies" for the ills that he saw in the current society.[58] The Celebrezze-labor cooperation did not interfere with socially conservative decisions that were an expression of his yearning "for an America . . . of high minded moralists, hard working and independent."[59] This overt moralism that was reflected in his restrained decision making in social issue cases gave rise to a reputation for conservatism. A political observer opined that "(h)e is conservative as a northern Democrat can get."[60] These two facets of his political personality, pro-labor, urban populism with a strong dash of middle-class social morality, explain the unbalanced record of activist decision making of the court under his leadership. The economic liberalism and social conservatism that drove his court was the outline of a gubernatorial platform that "would reach out to and cut across many constituencies and voting blocs."[61]

Frank Celebrezze was generally recognized as the leader of "his" court, the Ohio court majority composed of the other Democratic justices. Justice Clifford Brown expressed the Democratic members' feelings for their chief in remarks he delivered to a meeting of the state bar association: "Frank Celebrezze is perhaps the best Chief Justice the Ohio Supreme Court has ever had. . . . His leadership . . . has rubbed off on all of us, his associate justices."[62] The early 1980s Court was consistently referred to as the "Celebrezze court" and "Frank Celebrezze's partisan ideology . . . spurred the change"[63] in the nature of decision making on that court.

Other Members of the Court

Democratic Judges. Justice Clifford Brown provides an exception to the justices' spare publication record. He wrote two articles for Ohio law journals. These articles are aggressively pro-labor, anti-business. He noted that the Celebrezze court had "shown sensitivity to the plight of the employee" and had "come a long way toward supporting the rights of workers."[64] Although the title of one of the articles is "Judicial Activism," it does not shed any light on his preferred judicial, as distinct from political, philosophy. In that article, Justice Brown failed to distinguish between judicial activism and liberalism ("a judicial activist, i.e., a judicial liberal") but did reveal a class-based view of judicial decision making: "The judicial conservative(s) purpose: to give short shrift to the rights of the common man and woman" and the judicial liberal's purpose (and his own) was "to make . . . advanced, enlightened and common sense precedents" that made the Ohio court "truly a people's court."[65] Justice Resnick, who joined the court in January, 1989, has advocated a judicial change from the common-law "reasonable person" test to a "reasonable woman" test for a court's evaluation of women's claims of sexual harassment in the law review of an Ohio law school.[66] Justice Locher described his criteria for considering discretionary appeals to the court in the same law review without indicating whether he believed that a court should actively make state policy.[67] The other Democratic judges, Herbert Brown, William Brown, James Celebrezze, and A. W. Sweeney, were without any publications outside their judicial duties.[68]

Republican Judges. While the Democratic Clifford Brown flaunted his class-based political philosophy and neglected to describe his judicial philosophy, the new court's Republican justices loudly proclaimed their judicial philosophy and suppressed their political philosophy. It is perhaps characteristic of their different positions and different constituencies: the working men and women wanted to hear from the Democrats that the court intended to change the decades of judicial neglect that they felt they had experienced while business longed to hear from the Republicans that the status quo was going to be maintained.

Chief Justice Moyer did not delay in making clear the difference between his predecessor's and his judicial philosophy: "(T)he new Chief Justice understands that judges are not legislators in robes . . . it is the legislative branch that is best suited to determine the policy of the law."[69] After being chief for ten years, Moyer continued to favor the legislature as the state's policy maker.[70] As befits a justice of a "partisan" court, one Republican expressed his judicial role philosophy in a political ad. In his 1984 judicial election campaign, future Justice Craig Wright "aired some tough television ads complaining of the court's attempts to 'legislate.'"[71] Republican Justice Holmes's background and consistent dissent from the court's activist decisions give solid evidence of his non-activist predilection. The position of the remaining Republican, Justice Douglas, in the activist-non-activist tension is uncertain. He received substantial electoral support from interests that are certainly opposed to judicial activism if it results in anti-business decisions. However, Justice Douglas has been activist in every case that had an activist potential in which he has participated from the time the Republicans regained a majority on the court in 1987 to 1991. Coincidentally and significantly, each of these cases has been an upperdog-underdog case in which the activist decision was also pro-worker. Toledo, Ohio, Justice Douglas's hometown, is a medium-large Ohio city that is dominated by the glass manufacturing industry and considered an union town. It is not an electoral arena in which a potential Republican candidate for mayor could afford to brag about a pro-business, conservative voting record. His apparent activism may be related to his political ambition, similar to that of Chief Justice Frank Celebrezze.

OHIO SUPREME COURT CASES, 1981–1991

1981–1986, Activism in Economic Cases

The Ohio court was in the second rank of state high court innovators.[72] The vanguard states in the tort revolution of the 1960s and 1970s had excised from their jurisprudence the disqualifying common-law immunity doctrines. In the first half of the 1980s, the Ohio court caught up with a vengeance. In just four years, 1982 to 1985, the Court abrogated sovereign immunity,[73] interspousal immunity,[74] parental immunity,[75] and charitable immunity,[76] thereby wiping out the foundations of traditional common-law tort jurisprudence.

The Ohio court's attention to the interests of the Ohio working man and woman, led by its chief justice, channeled its activism into economic rather than social regulation. The common-law of Ohio had the full range of doctrine that traditionally protected governments, parents, spouses, and charities from liability for the injuries they caused. The new Celebrezze court decided the controversial cases that its predecessors had avoided and eliminated these traditional common-law immunities, which allowed the costs of an injury to be transferred from an underdog victim to an upperdog insurance carrier.

Workers' compensation was another fertile ground for the underdog's ambitious judicial champion. Smalltown and rural Ohio values and the business and industry orientation had shaped the Ohio court's approach to workers' compensation law during the seventy years since its adoption. The compromise between labor and industry on which workers' compensation was founded had prevented the injured workers from getting their cases to a jury and had limited their recovery to the schedule of benefits that the legislature had prescribed for work-related injuries. In a period of skyrocketing personal injury awards, this compromise seemed like a bad deal to the injured workers. They looked enviously at the increasingly generous juries and their employers' presumably deep pockets. Expeditiously, the Celebrezze court created an exception to the body of workers' compensation law that allowed injured workers to enjoy the juries' munificence if their employer had intentionally injured them.[77] The court's largess did not end when it opened the door for a worker to pursue the civil action pot of gold; it went further and allowed them to collect the scheduled workers' compensation benefits in addition to whatever a jury would give them in the civil action.[78]

Elimination of Traditional Doctrine and Rules. The judicial rules that the earlier Ohio courts had attached to the legislatively created workers' compensation had created a series of ever higher hurdles that the injured worker had to clear. These courts had adopted and approved judicial rules that had limited the right of workers to share in the compensation pool depending on the nature of the injury they suffered. Two of the rules that earlier Courts had engrafted on the system required that the worker suffer a physical injury and that the injury immediately follow the trauma that caused it. The post-1982 Ohio court overturned these venerable pillars of the Ohio workers' compensation system and held that workers could recover for mental or emotional injury that could be related to the job injury[79] and for an injury that had developed gradually over time as a result of job-related duties.[80] An earlier court had established a rule that a worker could not receive compensation for an injury received while traveling to or from the job. The Celebrezze court carved an exception that allowed the worker to receive compensation for an injury that occurred while the worker was turning into an employer's parking lot if the turn caused the employee to have a greater risk of injury than the general public. It then concluded that the necessity of regularly turning into the parking lot was such a greater risk![81]

Creation of New Causes of Action. The earlier Ohio courts had recognized only a limited number of tort causes of action and that had forced many injured Ohioans to bear the whole cost of their injuries if their cause had not been recognized. Every new cause of action that allows the responsibility to be transferred makes it likely that the cost will be transferred from the person injured to an insurance carrier who will spread the cost among the large number of its policy holders. The Celebrezze court accelerated its predecessors' deliberate pace in recognizing new torts that allowed individual responsibility to be transferred. Chief Justice Celebrezze proclaimed that "Ohio is rapidly being recognized as a national leader in providing appropriate remedies to meet the . . . issues . . . (of) modern society."[82]

Historically, a person could not maintain a civil action for emotional injury unless there was also physical injury. In 1983, the court overruled the controlling 1908 case to allow recovery for emotional injury that is unrelated to a physical injury.[83] The court created a cause of action for parents when negligent injury causes an otherwise viable fetus to be stillborn.[84] Physicians, particularly obstetricians, and their malpractice insurance carriers were the immediate victims of this new right to sue, but automobile insurance companies were similarly threatened. The court shifted the economic burden of the tragedy of the adoption of a seriously handicapped and impaired infant from the adopting parents by allowing them to sue the adoption agency for damage caused by a misrepresentation of the infant's background and condition.[85]

The court overruled the long-standing common-law principle that railroads do not have a duty to give warning to the public of a locomotive at a highway crossing.[86] Railroads, the historic adversary of the working man, were a likely target for the "people's court." The creation of the railroads' duty to warn motorists concomitantly created a cause of action against the offending railroad for the motorist who was injured at an unguarded crossing.

During the early 1980s, the Ohio General Assembly passed a law that eliminated the tort defense of contributory negligence and adopted comparative negligence for Ohio. When the Ohio court was presented with a case that had occurred prior to the legislation's effective date, which made the legislation unavailing to the plaintiff, the court didn't let the effective date of the law stand in its way; it found that comparative negligence was the common-law of Ohio for cases that arose prior to the legislation's effective date.[87] Although the life of this judicial comparative negligence was attenuated and therefore did not have the significance of the West Virginia court's similar decision, it did have a redistributive effect during the period in which it was applicable.

Statutes of Limitations. The traditional interpretation of statutes of limitations for actions involving physical injury required that a case be filed within a legislatively prescribed period of time that began to run at the time the act that caused the injury occurred, the time of injury rule. This judicial interpretation caused problems for plaintiffs in medical malpractice cases because the damaged patients frequently continued as a patient of the offending physicians past the time of the period and continued to trust them. The "time of injury" rule was also particularly harsh for asbestosis sufferers because the slow development of that condition would almost always outlast the statutory period. In response to these hardships, the Celebrezze court adopted a rule that the statute of limitations for medical malpractice actions[88] and for asbestosis related actions[89] began to run when the injured party discovered or reasonably should have discovered the injury, the "discovery rule." The court considered that a statute of limitations that incorporated the "time of injury" rule was not fair and held it unconstitutional.[90] When the Ohio General Assembly failed to promptly adopt a general statute of limitations for actions by minors after the court's decision that struck down the legislature's original statute, the court itself drafted and prescribed a "fair" judicial statute of limitations.[91]

Utility Rates. The court refused to allow utility companies to make consumers pay for programs that did not benefit them directly. The court said "no" when an electric company attempted to pass on to its customers the costs of an abandoned nuclear power plant.[92] When another public utility tried to force its customers to reimburse it for its charitable contributions, the court, similarly, protected the Ohio consumers.[93] In its most direct redistributive effort and one of the most publicized judicial incidents of the Celebrezze court's years, the chief justice literally redistributed the wealth. To effectuate a court order that directed public utility companies to make refunds to its customers, the court collected the refunds from the utility and then Celebrezze sent the customers their shares of the refund by checks over his own signature and in court envelopes.[94]

1981–1987, Restraint in Social Issue Cases

The 1980s decisions of the Ohio Supreme Court while Frank Celebrezze was chief justice in cases that had an activist potential can be neatly divided into two groups: activist decisions in which economic issues were joined and court activism would benefit working men and women and non-activist decisions in cases in which social issues were in the balance and the activist decision would have threatened family values. There is one case that falls outside this dichotomy. In that case the court overruled the common-law disqualification of a spouse's testimony in a criminal trial. This activist decision defies categorization: it was outside the activism pattern of the Celebrezze court because it was not redistributive, it threatened the stability of marriage, the court's opinion was written by Republican Justice Krupansky, the majority needed two Republican justice's votes, and Chief Justice Celebrezze dissented.[95] With the exception of this case, however, the Celebrezze court did not reach activist decisions if doing so would have offended the social values of the working men and women voters of Ohio.

It is generally believed that these Middle America voters valued local control of their public schools, supported police and law enforcement generally, and supported charitable causes. The average Ohioan was not thought to be sympathetic to feminist defenses of wives who killed their husbands, or criminals escaping "justice" on legal technicalities or by psychiatric excuse, and they believed that the state should do whatever was necessary to prevent the sexual exploitation of their sons and daughters. The decisions of the traditionalist Ohio court prior to 1978 were compatible with these voter's values and the Celebrezze-led Ohio court would do nothing to disturb them.

Criminal Law. The Celebrezze court demonstrated most clearly the similarity of its approach to social issues cases to that of its predecessor courts in the area of criminal law. The Celebrezze court's most interesting deference to the working voter's values and rejection of activism was its refusal to allow the admission of expert testimony to establish the "battered wife syndrome" defense to a murder charge against the wife.[96] The court's traditionalistic decision angered the women's movement, a vocal, though relatively small, component of Ohio's Democrat electoral coalition. It did not, however, disappoint the solid, conservative Ohio Democrat voter, a less vocal, but more numerous, electoral factor that was the heart of Frank Celebrezze's gubernatorial strategy. In other non-activist decisions, the court refused to invalidate an Ohio law that effectively denied criminal defendants their constitutionally guaranteed right to face their accuser;[97] allowed a prosecutor to use wiretap evidence that the police had obtained in violation of Ohio law;[98] refused to allow a severely mentally deficient defendant to use this "diminished capacity" as a defense to a criminal charge; and, not surprisingly, refused to protect the First Amendment right of privacy of a defendant who was caught with photographs of minors engaged in sexual activity in violation of Ohio law.[99] The votes of criminal defendants and their supporters do not decide elections.

Other Middle Class Values. The court did not embrace the "New Federalism" and did not utilize the Ohio Constitution's guarantee of a "thorough and efficient" system of schools to equalize educational funding in the state's poorer public school districts, although it recognized that their educational opportunities were unequal. It specifically relied on the middle-class "value of local control of schools."[100] In another activist decision the court joined its redistributive efforts and sensitivity to the values of the ordinary voter when it invalidated an Ohio statute that codified the common-law rule of mortmain.[101] The court's decision allowed a charity rather than a testator's heirs to receive property that the testator had left to it. The court preferred the redistributive effect of charitable giving to the enrichment of heirs.

In a balance between the redistributive effects of the creation of a new cause of action and the solid middle-class value of the rights of property, the court came down on the side of the middle-class Ohio voters' values. It refused to recognize that trespassers have a cause of action against property owners when they are injured by an artificial condition that the owners of the property maintain on their property, such as a swimming pool.[102] The court preferred to let property owners enjoy their land free of any obligation to unlawful intruders rather than force them to protect themselves by purchasing liability insurance. There are, undoubtedly, more Ohio property owners than Ohio plaintiffs.

1987–1991, Activism Moderated

The judicial election of 1986 returned control of the Ohio court to the Republicans, four–three. Chief Justice Celebrezze was replaced by Republican Thomas Moyer, while an incumbent Republican justice was reelected and one Democrat Brown, Herbert, replaced another, Clifford. This election continued the reversal of Democrat fortunes that had begun with the 1984 election in which the two Republican candidates, Craig Wright and Andy Douglas, had defeated incumbent Democrats, James Celebrezze, the Chief Justice's brother, and a Democrat candidate with the surname of a former Republican justice.[103] See Table 4.1. The 1984 and 1986 election campaigns were exceptional for Supreme Court races in Ohio: candidates attacked each other personally, the candidates were uniquely visible as a result of extensive media coverage, and the candidates spent large amounts of money, particularly in 1986. Much of both campaigns was waged over the direction the court's decisions had taken and the proper role of the Ohio court in policy making.[104]

The reestablishment of a Republican majority with substantial financial electoral support from interests that had suffered as a result of the activist decisions by the Democrats[105] led to speculation that the new court would institute wholesale reversal of the changes wrought by its predecessor. This did not happen.[106] The Moyer court initially chipped away at the abrasive edges of several of the

Celebrezze court innovations to make them more acceptable to the business interests that had helped it to get elected. The new court was not receptive when new causes of action were advocated. However, the new chief justice, Moyer, did not have the control over the post-1986 court that Celebrezze had over his court.[107] The new Ohio court would embrace activism as often as it rejected it. When it did, its range of activism was broader than its predecessor and included both economic and social cases. It was not obliging when the general assembly attempted to reduce the amount of potential recovery in tort actions and it did reverse the decision of its predecessor and came down on the side of protection of the interests of abused wives that the Celebrezze court had ignored

Economic Cases. In response to the Celebrezze court's decision allowing workers to maintain civil suits against their employers for intentional torts, the Ohio General Assembly had amended the workers' compensation law to require injured workers to bring these actions within the workers' compensation system.[108] The new court refused to allow an injured worker who had received an award against his employer in a civil suit to collect the award from the workers' compensation fund.[109] This generally pro-business decision was followed shortly by a pro-labor decision in which the court invalidated the legislature's attempt to force workers to try their intentional tort claims in the workers' compensation system with its low maximum recovery rather than to a civil jury with the potential for a bonanza. The court concluded that a suit for intentional tort was a common-law action, rather than a workers' compensation matter and threw out the legislature's attempt to limit recovery.[110]

The explosive upward spiral of judgments against health care providers in medical malpractice cases had sent them and their insurers to the legislature for relief. The Ohio General Assembly had responded to these organized cries by placing a cap of $200,000 on medical malpractice jury awards. Similar to its reaction to the legislature's attempt to limit recovery for an intentional tort, the court responded by tearing the cap off and decided that the limitation was unreasonable, arbitrary, and unconstitutional.[111]

The Celebrezze court had abrogated sovereign immunity except for governmental planning and policy-making activity.[112] The Moyer court made a slight retreat from it predecessor's activism and extended this limited immunity for a "reasonable time" after the government had made its policy decision in order to allow the policy to be implemented.[113] In its most pro-labor decision, the post-Celebrezze court freed Ohio workers from an assumption of the risks of their jobs. The common-law doctrine of assumption of risk included a corollary that provided that workers assumed the risks of injury that were necessarily encountered in the normal performance of their job duties and responsibilities. The post-1986 court abrogated this harsh, anti-labor doctrine,[114] but balanced its tilt toward the worker by getting rid of one of the Celebrezze court's anti-business workers' compensation decision. The Celebrezze court had allowed compensation for a worker who was injured while attempting to park in the employer's parking lot.[115] In 1991, the court overruled the Celebrezze precedent and excluded injuries workers suffered while parking. Democratic Judge, Herbert Brown, concluded that such risks were not greater than the general public encountered on crowded and congested streets.[116]

The Republican-controlled Ohio court hesitated to approve novel theories of relief. It refused to recognize a cause of action by a building contractor against an architect for economic damage suffered by the contractor as a result of the architect's faulty design. Its new legalistic majority relied on the lack of a contractual relationship between the contractor and the architect to refuse to find a cause of action in tort.[117] Similarly, it refused to recognize the controversial "clergy malpractice" cause of action when a divorced husband sought to collect damages from a clergyman who had sexual relations with his wife while he was acting as a marriage counselor for the couple.[118] The Ohio court found this cause of action too close to alienation of affection, an action that is in general disrepute. The non-activist approach to these cases was probably welcome to the Republicans' electoral supporters but it seems meager repayment, in itself. However, it is likely that the new Ohio court's business and other backers were satisfied that the activist Celebrezze court was now only a bad memory.

Although the post-1986 Ohio court was not as activist as its predecessor, during the period 1987 to 1991 it did reach significant activist decisions in five of ten cases that had an activist potential. One of its Republican members[119] joined the three Democratic members to remove a long-standing limitation on workers seeking compensation benefits. This bipartisan bloc overruled a seventy-one-year-old judicial rule that had denied workers' compensation benefits to the worker unless the injury had been caused by a work hazard that was "different or greater than the general public encounters."[120] Labor was undoubtedly pleased that another hurdle had been removed from the path of the injured worker and, on the other side of the coin, business must have been disappointed that a judge whom it had helped to elect had provided the necessary vote to their disadvantage.

After the flood tide of activism in the first half of the 1980s, activist decisions continued to flow from the court, but the stream returned to its banks after the Moyer court convened. In another activist decision the new court overruled the Celebrezze court and allowed the battered wife to introduce evidence of the "battered wife syndrome" to support a claim of self defense.[121] The court's protection of a battered wife's civil liberties would not have been of substantial interest to the big 1986 contributors on either side, but was unquestionably satisfying to militant women, perhaps a part of a future electoral majority.

The relationship between the Ohio court's activism and Frank Celebrezze, its activist advocate, was different from the Indiana–Shepard and West Virginia–Neely relationships. Unlike either of the other two activist advocates, the accession of Frank Celebrezze to his state's court did not elicit activist responses from the natural court[122] that he joined. It was not until fellow Democrats joined him on the court to create a Democratic majority that the court began its period of phenomenal activism. If Justice Celebrezze advocated activist decision making prior to 1979, his was a voice in a restrained wilderness. It is possible that his conservative political philosophy[123] was satisfied with traditional decision making until his gubernatorial ambition was ignited during his unsuccessful attempt to be the Democratic Party's endorsed candidate in its 1978 primary. This ambition, when joined with his election as chief justice in the subsequent general judicial election in that year and the election of a Democratic majority, gave him a prominence from which he could realistically take credit for the court's politically popular decisions. Prior to 1979, it would have been difficult for one lone Democrat associate justice out of seven to claim credit for judicially made policy. His election as chief made him, arguably, the highest ranking Ohio Democrat and the Democratic majority on the court made him the chief of a court whose majority's policy preferences would appeal to Ohio Democrats. When the court's chief justice who is the acknowledged leader of the court's Democrat majority,[124] claims credit for popular policy, such claim becomes credible.

Except in the aberrational case that made a change in the common-law to allow a wife to testify against her husband in the husband's criminal prosecution,[125] Celebrezze was a member of the majority in every case in which the Court was asked to be an independent policy maker during the period 1981 to 1986. The court's Democratic majority supported their chief, both when he made activist policy in economic cases as well as when he declined and affirmed the status quo in social issue cases.

Unlike the Indiana and West Virginia courts that included the activist advocate during the full ten-year period of our consideration, with the Ohio court we can assess the court's activism after the activist advocate has left the court. Frank Celebrezze's defeat in the chief justice election of 1986 removed him from the court. Judicial activism, nevertheless, continued in the post 1986 Ohio court, albeit at a lower, but still significant level without his advocacy. The post-1986 court was decidedly bi-polar with the three minority Democratic justices making activist decisions and three of the four Republican justices continuing the traditional non-active course. The legitimacy that partisan political judicial activism had achieved under the leadership of Chief Justice Celebrezze survived its master in some form, at least with the Democratic justices. Chief Justice Celebrezze had interrupted the Ohio court's traditional jurisprudential repose to serve his political purpose; he had mustered a majority from his fellow Democratic justices for activist decisions in the economic issues cases. The addition of activist decisions in social issues cases by the post-1986 court to the economic issues cases that were the limit of the Celebrezze court's activism may have signaled a change from the partisan political activism of the Celebrezze court to ideological activism. The genie of judicial activism, once freed from its master's political bottle, mutated to serve the ideological preferences of the court's 1987–1990 majority. The influence of the activist advocacy that Frank Celebrezze had on the Ohio Supreme Court survived his defeat, but in a different guise.

NOTES

1. Michael Barone and Grant Ujifusa, *The Almanac of American Politics 1996* (Washington, D.C.: National Journal, 1995), p. 1028.

2. Barone and Ujifusa, *1996*, p. 1028. The previous sixteen had either been English colonies or were created from former colonies.

3. Barone and Ujifusa, *1996*, p. 1028.

4. No Republican president has been elected without Ohio's electoral votes. Barone and Ujifusa, *1996*, p. 1030.

5. Barone and Ujifusa, *1996*, p. 1028. "Normalcy" is a word that was apparently given acceptability by its repeated use by Ohioan Warren G. Harding in his 1920 presidential campaign. The scandals during Harding's subsequent presidency and the "the Ohio gang" put an end to Ohio's presidential successes.

6. Kathleen L. Barber, "Ohio Judicial Elections—Non-partisan Premises with Partisan Results," *Ohio State Law Journal* 32 (1971): 726–789. Progressives prescribed the partisan primary as the vehicle for nomination of all elected officers, including judges, in order to avoid the selection of candidates by political bosses; they chose a non-partisan contest for final selection in order to eliminate the "non-democratic" influence of partisan politics.

7. G. Alan Tarr and Mary Cornelia Porter, *State Supreme Courts in State and Nation* (New Haven, Conn.: Yale University Press, 1989), p. 126.

8. Barber, "Ohio Judicial Elections."

9. Barber, "Ohio Judicial Elections," p. 728. Barber later explained this phenomenon by the characteristics of the Republican voter: relatively higher income and more education, which leads them to vote in the remote, low information and relatively clueless nonpartisan judicial election. Their greater education enables them to more readily develop cues that enable them to identify the Republican candidates. Kathleen L. Barber, "Judicial Politics in Ohio," in *Government and Politics in Ohio*, Carl Lieberman, ed. (Lanham, Md.: University Press of America, 1984), p. 14.

10. Just as it had the Indiana court.

11. Rodney L. Mott, "Judicial Influence," *American Political Science Review* 30 (1936): 295–315.

12. Gregory Caldeira, "On the Reputation of State Courts," *Political Behavior* 5 (1983): 83.

13. Bradley Cannon and Lawrence Baum, "Patterns of Adoption of Tort Law Innovations: an Application of Diffusion Theory to Judicial Doctrines," *American Political Science Review* 75 (1981): 975–987.

14. Barber, "Judicial Politics," p. 91.

15. After 1851, and until 1911–1912, the Ohio Supreme Court justices were nominated by party convention and elected in partisan elections; since the Ohio Constitutional Convention in 1912, they have been nominated in partisan primaries and elected in nonpartisan elections. Barber, "Judicial Politics," p. 91.

16. Tarr and Porter, *State Supreme Courts*, p. 127.

17. Tarr and Porter, *State Supreme Courts,* p. 127.

18. Barber, "Judicial Politics," p. 117.

19. Tarr and Porter report that a Democratic veteran member of the court with thirty-four years service on the court was frequently mistaken by his friends as a Republican. Tarr and Porter, *State Supreme Courts*, p. 140, n. 29.

20. Tarr and Porter, *State Supreme Courts,* p. 127, n. 5.

21. Barber, "Judicial Politics," p. 110.

22. Sweeneys had run on the statewide ballot repeatedly in the 1960s for attorney general and congress-at-large; Frank Celebrezze ran for election to the Supreme Court four times and James Celebrezze once between 1972 and 1982; their uncle, Anthony J. Celebrezze, had been mayor of Ohio's largest city, Cleveland, Secretary of Health, Education and Welfare, and was a judge on the U.S. Circuit Court of Appeals and their cousin, Anthony Jr, (Tony), had been elected Ohio's Secretary of State and Attorney General; Brown was a popular name for Republican statewide candidates, probably because of the regular and popular candidacy of longtime Secretary of State, Ted W. Brown. The association of Supreme Court Justice Paul Brown with the popular Cleveland Browns and Cincinnati Bengals football coach of the same name undoubtedly added to his, and the name's, popularity.

23. Tarr and Porter, *State Supreme Courts,* p. 129.

24. "Attractive nuisance" is a pro-plaintiff doctrine that enables a plaintiff to maintain an action against the owner of a "nuisance" that attracts the plaintiff onto the owners property and results in the plaintiff's injury. A pool is an example of an attractive nuisance, although not all states that recognize the doctrine would apply it to pools.

25. Tarr and Porter, *State Supreme Courts.*

26. Ohio Revised Code, Sec. 2503.02.

27. The court must hear direct appeals from decisions of the state's Board of Tax Appeals and Public Utilities Commission, and trial courts in cases in which the death sentence has been ordered.

28. *State Caseload Statistics: Annual Report 1986* (National Center for State Courts, Court Statistics and Information Project, July, 1988), pp. 121, 123, and 125.

29. Ohio Revised Code, Sec. 2503.02.

30. The justices biographical information is found in various editions of *The American Bench, Judges of the Nation* (Sacramento, Calif.: Forster-Long, Inc).

31. Democrats: William B. Brown, Harvard; Herbert Brown, Michigan; Clifford Brown, Notre Dame; A. W. Sweeney, Duke. Republican: Craig Wright, Harvard.

32. Democrats: Frank and James Celebrezze and Ralph Locher, Cleveland; William B. Brown, Honolulu, Hawaii; Alice Resnick, Toledo; A. W. Sweeney, Youngstown; Herbert R. Brown, Columbus. Republicans: Paul W. Brown, Youngstown; Andy Douglas, Toledo; Blanche Krupansky, Cleveland; Robert Holmes, Thomas Moyer and Craig wright, Columbus. The exception was Clifford

Brown who practiced law from 1938 to 1964 in Norwalk, Ohio, a community of about 40,000.

33. Paul Brown, 1970; Frank Celebrezze, 1982.

34. Ralph Locher had been Secretary to Governor Frank Lausche and Thomas Moyer had been Administrative Assistant to Governor James Rhodes. Although the title had been changed, they performed the same function, that of personal counsel and chief of staff, and, in fact, their offices occupied the same space in the governor's suite of offices.

35. Paul W. Brown, 1969–1971.

36. Ralph Locher, Mayor; Frank Celebrezze, candidate.

37. Frank Celebezze, Ohio Senate; Robert Holmes, Majority Leader and Speaker of the House of Representatives.

38. William B. Brown, 1949.

39. Andy Douglas, Toledo.

40. Democrats A. W. Sweeney and Herbert R. Brown were elected to the high court on their initial venture into politics.

41. Kathleen L. Barber, "Judicial Politics in Ohio," in *Government and Politics in Ohio*, Carl Lieberman, ed. (Lanham, Md.: University Press of America, 1984).

42. Justice Herbert's father, Paul Herbert, had been elected lieutenant governor in the 1950s and to the court in the 1960s. Another Herbert, Thomas, had been elected governor of Ohio in 1946, and had run, unsuccessfully, in 1948 for reelection, before being elected an associate justice of the court. Governor Herbert's son, John, had been elected treasurer of state twice in the 1960s and had been the Republican candidate for attorney general in 1970. Thomas Herbert had been elected to the Ohio Senate before twice being elected associate justice.

43. John Fenton, *Midwest Politics* (New York: Holt, Rinehart and Winston, 1966), p. 153.

44. The Ohio State Bar Association ethics committee investigated the propriety of Chief Justice Celebrezze remaining on the court after he had "announced his intention to run for governor." Ohio had adopted Canon 7(A)(3) of the American Bar Association that provides: "A judge should resign his office when he becomes a candidate in a party primary or in a general election for nonjudicial office." Celebrezze had announced that he intended to run for governor in January 1982, but continued to act as a member of the court during January, February, and until March 10 when he submitted his resignation. Gail Appleson, "'Resign-to-Run' Canon Faces Test in Ohio," *American Bar Association Journal* 68 (May, 1982): 535.

45. Tarr and Porter, *State Supreme Courts*, p. 132. The chief justice supported his brother's candidacy, which was successful in 1982.

46. *Columbus and Southern Ohio Electric Co. v. Public Utilities Commission of Ohio*, 460 N.E.2d 1108 (1984).

47. Tarr and Porter, *State Supreme Courts,* p. 134. It was assumed that Frank Celebrezze intended that the court's checks with the Celebrezze name would

benefit James Celebrezze's candidacy. If they did, it was not enough; James lost to the Republican, Craig Wright. The chief justice's fellow Democratic justice, Ralph Locher, believed that this ploy Alargely led to (James') defeat." Roger K. Lowe, "Locher Set To Enter Retirement Looks Back On 43-Year Career," *Columbus Dispatch*, December 26, 1988, p. 3B.

48. Mary Ann Sharkey and W. Steven Ricks, "A Law Unto Himself: Chief Justice appears to ignore judicial code," *Plain Dealer*, Apr. 26, 1984, p. 27A.

49. Mary Ann Sharkey, "Celebrezze Longs for Acceptance," *The Plain Dealer*, April 23, 1983.

50. Sharkey, "Celebrezze Longs for Acceptance."

51. Steven Avorkian, quoted in Mary Ann Sharkey and W. Steven Ricks, "A Law Unto Himself," *The Plain Dealer*, April 26, 1984, p. 20A.

52. The Hon. Frank Celebrezze, "The Supreme Court of Ohio," *Ohio Northern Law Review* XII (1985): xiii.

53. Celebrezze's populism was focused largely on urban and labor concerns. His social conservatism had an appeal to both urban workers and the rural Roman Catholic Democratic voter in Ohio's Northwest.

54. *New York Times*, October 14, 1984, Sec. 1, p. 35. The *New York Times* reported that Celebrezze had said that the court's "populists decisions had favored common people as opposed to 'special vested interests.'"

55. The Hon. Frank Celebrezze, "The Supreme Court of Ohio 1983–1984 Term," *Ohio Northern University Law Review* XI (1984): xv.

56. *Blankenship v. Cincinnati Milicron Chemicals, Inc.*, 433 N.E.2d 572 (1982). In a Petition for Rehearing, counsel for the employer, Cincinnati Milicron Chemicals, Inc., described Celebrezze's opinion in that case as a "politically oriented message to Ohioans from a man who had publicly stated seven weeks earlier that he wants to be governor." Appleson, *"'Resign-to-Run.'"*

57. Kathleen L. Barber, "Judicial Politics in Ohio."

58. Plain Dealer, Feb. 3, 1979, p. 1A.

59. Charles Stella, "The Celebrezze Dynasty," *The Plain Dealer*, April 24, 1983, p. 32.

60. Stella, "The Celebrezze Dynasty."

61. Tarr and Porter, *State Supreme Courts.*

62. The Hon. Clifford F. Brown, "Practice Before the Supreme Court of Ohio: Oral Argument." *Ohio State Bar Association Report* 58 (June 10,1985): 952–954.

63. Tarr and Porter, *State Supreme Courts,* p. 183.

64. The Hon. Clifford F. Brown, "The Trend of Worker's Compensation in Ohio: Ohio Puts the Worker Back in Worker's Compensation," *Capitol University Law Review* 13 (1984): 521.

65. The Hon. Clifford F. Brown, "Judicial Activism," *Ohio Northern University Law Review* XIII (1987): 157.

66. The Hon. Alice Robie Resnick, "The Reasonable Woman Standard," *Ohio Northern Law Review* 19 (1992): 17. Justice Resnick also contributed an essay

in which she advocated action to eliminate gender bias from the legal profession, "The Essence of Gender Fairness," *Ohio Northern Law Review* 19 (1993): 549 and a Preface to an annual summary of the Ohio court's cases, *Ohio Northern Law Review* 23 (1996): 421.

67. The Hon. Ralph S. Locher, "A Supreme Court Justice's Perspective on Discretionary Appeals" *Ohio Northern Law Review* 12 (1985): 301. Justice Locher wrote that "(j)udicial consistency is . . . important as an end in itself" and also that "the law is always in a state of flux."

68. Justice Herbert Brown has written two novels.

69. The Hon. Thomas R. Moyer, "The Supreme Court of Ohio: Restoration of an Institution," *Ohio State Bar Association Report* 60 (Jan. 6,1987): 84. Justice Moyer has also written a history of the Bill of Rights, "The Bill of Rights-Its Origins and Its Keepers" *Judicature* 75 (Aug.-Sept., 1991): 57 and an essay advocating the use of alternative dispute resolution as an alternative to confrontation in settlement of interpersonal disputes, "Essay: ADR As an Alternative to Our Culture of Confrontation," *Cleveland State Law Review* 43 (1995): 13. In neither does he give a further indication of his preferred judicial role.

70. Darrel Rowland, "Politics Not a Key Factor in Decision," *Columbus Dispatch,* March 25, 1997, p. 1E.

71. "Politics Defeats Two Democrat Justices," *The Los Angeles Daily Journal* 97 (Nov. 8,1986): 5.

72. Bradley Canon and Lawrence Baum, APatterns of Adoption," p. 975–987.

73. *Havelock v. Portage Homes, et al.*, 442 N.E.2d 749 (1982)—municipal corporations; *Corlone v. Oberfield*, 451 N.E.2d 1229 (1983)—school boards; but see *Enghouser Manufacturing Company v. Erikson Engineering, Ltd.*, 451 N.E.2d 228 (1983), in which the Ohio court limited its abrogation.

74. *Prem v. Cox*, 443 N.E.2d 511 (1982)—workers' compensation; *Shearer v. Shearer*, 480 N.E.2d (1984)—civil action.

75. *Kirchner v. Chrystal*, 474 N.E.2d 275 (1984).

76. *Albritton v. Neighborhood Centers Association,* 466 N.E.2d 867 (1984).

77. *Blankenship v. Cincinnati Millicron Chemicals, Inc.*, 433 N.E.2d 572 (1982); *State, ex rel. Nytray v. Industrial Commission*, 443 N.E.2d 962 (1983).

78. *Jones v. V.I.P. Development Company*, 472 N.E.2d 1046 (1984).

79. *Ryan v. Connor*, 503 N.E.2d 570 (1986).

80. *Ryan v. Connor*, 503 N.E.2d 1379 (1986).

81. *Littlefield v. Pillsbury Co.*, 453 N.E.2d 570 (1983).

82. The Hon. Frank Celebrezze, "The Supreme Court," *Ohio Northern Law Review* XII (1985): xiii.

83. *Schultz v. Barberton Glass Company*, 447 N.E.2d 109 (1983).

84. *Werling v. Sandy, et al.*, 476 N.E.2d 1053 (1983).

85. *Burr v. Board of Commissioners, et al.*, 491 N.E.2d 1101 (1986).

86. *Matkovich v. Penn Central Transportation Company*, 431 N.E.2d 652 (1982).

87. *Wilfong v. Batdorf*, 451 N.E.2d 1185 (1983). See, *Viers v. Dunlap,*

438 N.E.2d 881 (1982), decided a year earlier and before Justice Krupansky, who was in the majority in *Viers*, was replaced on the court by James Celebrezze, who was in the majority in *Wilfong*.

88. *Oliver v. Kaiser Community Health Foundation*, 449 N.E.2d 438 (1983).

89. *O'Stricker v. Jim Walter Corp.*, 447 N.E.2d 727 (1983).

90. *ID v. Riverside Methodist Hospital*, 503 N.E.2d 1337 (1986).

91. *Mominee et al. v. Scherbarth et al.*, 503 N.E.2d 717 (1986).

92. *Office of Consumer Counsel v. Public Utilities* Commission, *et al.*, 423 N.E. 820 (1980).

93. *City of Cleveland v. Public Utility Commission, et al.*, 406 N.E.2d 1370 (1980).

94. Court ordered refunds were not unique; the personalization of the method of refund was.

95. *State v. Mowery*, 438 N.E.2d 897 (1982).

96. *State v. Thomas*, 423 N.E.2d 137 (1981).

97. *State v. Madison*, 415 N.E.2d 272 (1980). The statute in question, Section 2945.49, Ohio Revised Code, allows recorded testimony to be admitted in a criminal trial if the accuser is not available at trial. See Ohio Constitution, Section 10, Article I.

98. *State v. Geraldo*, 429 N.E.2d 141 (1981); see Section 4931.28, Ohio Revised Code.

99. *State v. Meadows*, 503 N.E.2d 697 (1986). This decision was announced twenty-four days before the 1986 judicial election in which the chief justiceship and two other Democrat seats were at stake. Although the decision is not inconsistent with the court's pattern, its timing probably eliminated any vestige of hope the defendant had.

100. *Board of Education etc., et al. v. Walter*, 390 N.E.2d 813 (1979).

101. Mortmain is, literally, "dead hand" and refers to the potential control of most real property in a country by a pervasive charity, such as the Roman Catholic Church in pre-Reformation England, and the fear that this caused the civil government. In order to reduce this potential threat, various restrictions were imposed on charitable property rights under the general designation, mortmain. The Ohio statute in question, Section 2107.06, Ohio Revised Code, invalidated charitable bequests that had been made shortly before the testator's death. The legislature repealed this statute while the case was pending in the court.

102. *Elliott v. Nagy*, 488 N.E.2d 853 (1986). This is an Aattractive nuisance" case. An attractive nuisance is an artificial condition that exists on real property that lures trespassers on to the property and then causes their injury.

103. Although the name was the same as the previous Republican justice, it was a name, Corrigan, that many voters, particularly in populous Cuyahoga County, would think belonged to a Democrat. Thus is the Ohio "name game" confusing.

104. G. Alan Tarr and Mary Cornelia Porter, *State Supreme Courts in Nation and State* (New Haven: Yale University Press, 1989).

105. Lawrence Baum, "State Supreme Courts: Activism and Accountability," in *The State of the States*, Carl E. Van Horn, ed. (Washington, D.C.: CQ Press, 1989).

106. Although the election returned control of the court to Republican hands, the Republican majority was of only one justice, and one of the Republican justices, Andy Douglas, was a political moderate.

107. James Bradshaw, "Supreme Court Rejects 'Wrongful Life' Suit the Association Is Grateful the Court, By a 4-3 Vote, Did Not Allow a Hospital to be Sued for Saving a Life" *Columbus Dispatch*, October 11, 1996, p. 1C.

108. See *Blankenship v. Cincinnati Milicron*.

109. *State, ex rel., Carpenter v. Industrial Commission*, 552 N.E.2d 645 (1990).

110. *Brady v. Safety Kleen Corp.*, 576 N.E.2d 722 (1991).

111. *Morris v. Savoy*, 576 N.E.2d 765 (1991).

112. *Enghauser Manufacturing Company v. Ericsson Engineering Ltd.*.

113. *Garland v. Ohio Department of Transportation*, 548 N.E.2d 233 (1990).

114. *Cremeans v. Willmar Henderson Manufacturing Co.*, 566 N.E.2d 1203 (1991).

115. See *Littlefield v. Pillsbury Co.*.

116. *M.T.D. Products, Inc. v. Robatin, et al.*, 572 N.E.2d 661 (1991).

117. *Floor Craft Floor Company, v. Parma Community General Hospital*, 560 N.E.2d 206 (1990).

118. *Strock v. Presnell*, 527 N.E.2d 1235 (1988).

119. Justice Douglas. Justice Douglas "frequently votes with Democrats on matters important to organized labor." James Bradshaw, "'Moyer Court' Changing Again Swing Votes Are Key in Ohio's Highest Judicial Body," *Columbus Dispatch*, June 19, 1994. Douglas is the "rare (Ohio) Republican who can count on substantial backing from labor unions." Darrel Rowland, "Politics Not a Factor in Decision," *Columbus Dispatch*, March 25, 1997, p. 1E. Douglas would need the unions' support if he ever became a candidate for mayor of his hometown, Toledo, Ohio, which he has reportedly considered. James Bradshaw, "2 Justices May be Pursuing Other Dreams," *Columbus Dispatch*, November 26, 1992, p. 3E.

120. *Griffin v. Hydra-Matic Division, etc.*, 529 N.E.2d 436 (1988).

121. *State v. Koss*, 551 N.E.2d 970 (1990). The Court still refused to recognize the "battered wife syndrome" as a new and separate defense.

122. "Natural court" is a phrase that describes a court during the period in which its membership does not change. The natural court that Frank Celebrezze joined in January 1973 continued until 1977 when William Sweeney and Ralph Locher joined the Ohio court, creating a new natural court. See Table 4.1.

123. Stella, "The Celebrezze Dynasty."

124. The Hon. Clifford F. Brown, "Practice."

125. *State v. Mowery*, 438 N.E.2d 897 (1982).

Chapter 5

Idaho, Florida, and Pennsylvania

During the 1970s and 1980s the Courts of Indiana, West Virginia, and Ohio were significant policy makers in their states. Each of these courts had a member who advocated that their court should intentionally and actively participate in its state's policy making. During comparable ten-year periods three other courts, those of Idaho, Florida, and Pennsylvania, did not make policy in their states nor did any of the three have a member who advocated that the court should intentionally and actively make state policy by its decisions. The following descriptions of these courts, their decision making and their judge's preferred judicial role, will enable a comparison to be made of the level of judicial policy making in courts with an activist advocate and its level in courts without such an advocate. Just as the states of Indiana, West Virginia, and Ohio, though contiguous, are decidedly disparate and their courts were significantly different, so are the geographically separated states of Idaho, Florida, and Pennsylvania geographically and economically dissimilar and their courts had different structures and characteristics.

IDAHO

Idaho Supreme Court Preferred Judicial Role

The justices who served on the Idaho Supreme Court during the 1980s received their legal education at Idaho law schools or at a local law school in the neighboring state of Washington. None attended a national law school. None directly addressed the question of the propriety of judicial activism in extra-judicial writing as Justices Shepard and Neely did. However, the glimpses that we have of their preferred judicial role, either incidentally in what they wrote or in the retrospection of others after their deaths, are consistent with their invocations in their opinions of legislative action to address current problems. Justice Bakes, who served on the court during the entire decade, in a speech to the Idaho Newspaper Association in 1988 equated judicial restraint with democracy and described judicial activism as undemocratic: "If the core value of the Constitution is democracy, then this core value is best preserved by judges practicing judicial restraint. Judicial lawmaking is essentially undemocratic. Judges are not elected by the popular majority based upon their platforms and promises on how they would decide future cases."[1] Justice Huntley wrote about a problem that he believed the Idaho court had created by its interpretation of Idaho's Tort Claims Act.[2] Rather than advocating a judicial solution for the problem he saw, Justice Huntley wrote that "if such a distinction needs to be made, it is best left for the legislature to make it."[3] Justice Donaldson advised the Idaho Bar Association that "if stability (in the law) is lacking, people can not predict the consequences of their actions."[4]

Justice Allen G. Shepard died while serving on the bench. Memorials by two of the judges of the court confirm Justice Shepard's dedication to restrained judicial decision making. Justice Byron Johnson remembered him as "somewhat doctrinaire and predictable" and an "advocate of stare decisis." Significantly, Justice Johnson indicated that he shared Justice Shepard's dedication to stare decisis.[5] Justice Bakes, who succeeded Justice Shepard, remembered that he had a "keen respect for the authority of the other two constitutional branches of government"[6]

Idaho Court System

The structure of the Idaho court system remained unchanged during the 1980s after July 1, 1981, the date on which Idaho's intermediate appellate court was established.[7] The Idaho court had five justices who were elected[8] in nonpartisan elections[9] for six-year terms.[10] The Idaho court's chief justice was chosen by the justices for a four-year term.[11]

Idaho Supreme Court Cases, 1980–1990

During the decade of the 1980s, the Idaho court was restrained in its decision making and generally refrained from participating in making public policy. When it discovered anomalies or unfairness in the operation of the established Idaho law, it looked to the Idaho legislature to rectify them. It hesitated to disturb the common-law doctrines that had been established by earlier Idaho courts and in the one case in which it did modify a common-law doctrine it did so grudgingly. When the court created a new cause of action, it gave the injured Idaho plaintiffs substantially less than they sought and less than plaintiffs had gotten from other state courts.

Uninsured Motorists. The Idaho court's cases interpreting the Idaho uninsured motorist coverage statute[12] exemplify its preferred restrained judicial role. The Idaho legislature had followed the trend in the states and had enacted an uninsured motorist coverage statute. This law required automobile insurance companies that did business in Idaho to make insurance protection against uninsured motorists available to Idaho insurers. The purpose of this law was to protect innocent victims "from irresponsible drivers who cannot indemnify such victims from the harm their conduct causes."[13] During the 1980s, the court had repeated occasion to interpret this law and uniformly demonstrated its preferred restrained judicial role by deferring to the legislature, regardless of the court's view of the wisdom of the legislative policy. The court's deference favored the insurance companies and hurt the insured victim in disregard of the law's purpose. The Idaho cases reveal that there were three unanswered questions inherent in the Idaho law as enacted by the Idaho legislature: what was the effect of a uninsured motorist coverage policy when injury has been caused by an *underinsured* motorist;[14] what was the effect of a provision in an uninsured motorist coverage policy that excluded coverage when the insured is injured when driving a vehicle that he/she owns other than the one described in the policy; and what was the effect of an uninsured coverage policy when the insured party is injured by an unidentified "hit-and-run" driver that had not come in physical contact with the insured or the insured's vehicle? In each case in which these questions were presented to the Idaho court, the court's decision denied recovery to the victim who had purchased uninsured motorist coverage.

The Idaho court refused to develop a general policy for the uninsured motorist coverage law when it considered two cases in the middle of the decade in which the drivers who caused the injury each had liability insurance, but in an amount that was insufficient to pay for the damage they had caused—underinsured motorists. The Arizona and Hawaii legislatures had enacted uninsured motorist coverage laws similar to Idaho's and, in cases similar to the Idaho cases, the Arizona and Hawaii courts had held that the underinsured motorist was "uninsured" and they had permitted recovery of the difference between the amount available from the insurance of the underinsured motorist who had caused the injury and the limits of the uninsured motorist coverage policy. The Idaho court did not follow the trail the Arizona and Hawaii courts had forged but in these two cases held that Idaho's law did not allow the victim to recover anything on their uninsured motorist coverage policy. In the first case, the Idaho court recognized that its decision was "inequitable" but refused to "make a decision of policy" because "all such questions should be dealt with by a legislative body. . . . Again, we urge legislative attention."[15] In the second case, the court concluded that "(n)either the Idaho legislature nor the courts have declared that there exists a public policy applicable to *under-insured* motorist coverage. While such policy might be desirable . . . that public policy should be enunciated by our legislature and not this Court."[16]

Automobile insurance companies regularly excluded coverage under uninsured motorist coverage policies for injuries suffered when the insured was driving a vehicle owned by him/her but other than the one described in the policy. When the Idaho court considered the effect of this exclusionary language, it allowed it to effectively deny recovery to the insured even though this decision created the anomalous situation that the injured insured would have a claim under the uninsured motorist coverage policy if injured by an uninsured motorist while driving a borrowed vehicle or while walking but not when driving his/her own vehicle. The court could find "no public policy implicit in our statutory scheme of automobile insurance" and ignored this opportunity to fill the void with judicially made policy.[17] The court's restraint allowed the anomaly to continue and denied insurance protection to Idaho motorists.

The Idaho court allowed another anomaly to develop when it permitted insurance companies to exclude from uninsured motorist coverage damage that results from a "hit-and run" accident in which the hit-and-run vehicle had not come in contact with the insured vehicle.[18] In his dissent, Justice Bistline, who would have allowed the insured to collect despite an uninsured motorist policy's exclusionary language, pointed out that "victims of hit-and run drivers who were skillful and careful enough to avoid contact . . . ironically would be left without coverage." Justice Bistline recognized that "growing number of courts . . . have found that the physical contact requirement violated the intent of (the uninsured motorist coverage) statutes."[19]

Modification of the Common Law. The court was especially restrained when it was asked to create common-law causes of action or to modify existing common-law doctrine to make it easier for Idaho plaintiffs to recover for their injuries. The traditional common-law of torts distinguished between "trespassers" on private property and those who were on property as "licensees" or "invitees." This common-law distinction required a property owner only to refrain from wilful and wanton acts against a trespasser but to exercise "reasonable care" to avoid injury to the nontrespasser. Idaho had maintained the common-law distinction that substantially reduced the opportunity for compensation for wrongfully caused injuries. The trend in state courts has been to abolish the distinction and to allow an injured person, whether or not a trespasser, to successfully maintain an action against a property owner who failed to exercise reasonable care for his/her safety. The Idaho court refused to follow this trend to ameliorate the harsh effect of the common-law rule and continued to deny a cause of action for injury caused by a property owner's ordinary negligence to one who happened to be on property without the owner's invitation.[20]

The Idaho common law allowed compensation for physical injury that had been caused by negligence but did not provide compensation for economic injury that had been caused by negligence. The 1980s Idaho court refused to broaden this common-law rule when it was presented a case in which the owner of an apartment building suffered loss of rental income and the cost of repairing a building that had been negligently constructed. The court refused to allow the owner to sue the negligent contractor for those losses that the contractor's negligence had caused.[21] The Idaho common-law had another limitation on the right of a person who had been injured by another's negligence to maintain an action for the resulting injury. Idaho law continued the traditional common-law rule that there was no cause of action for recovery for negligently caused emotional injury unless the negligence had also caused some physical injury. The Idaho court disallowed an action by a person who had suffered severe emotional distress as a result of an airplane crash landing that had been caused by negligent maintenance and repair of the airplane.[22]

The Idaho court was no more sympathetic when asked to create new common-law causes of action. The court refused to enlarge the Idaho common-law to allow an injured person to maintain a cause of action against the owner of an automobile who had left the keys in the automobile's ignition, enabling an apparent "joy rider" to use the automobile to cause the injury.[23] The court denied the right to maintain an action, although the plaintiff had argued that the owner should be responsible for the injury because he had violated Idaho law by leaving the keys in the car's ignition[24] and had thereby implicitly consented to the use of the automobile.

The Idaho court denied a property owner the right to maintain an action against the state that had substantially reduced a property owner's access to the public streets when it had created a limited access highway.[25] A dissenting justice observed that "we must assume that the value of . . . (the owner's) property has been severely diminished by the action of the State."[26] Nevertheless, the Idaho court concluded that such a reduction of access is not such a taking of property that would allow the property owner to maintain an action against the state for the reduction in value.

Reluctant Change. Decisions of the Idaho court during the 1980s that appear to be activist, declaring laws passed by the legislature unconstitutional, overruling its own decisions, and creating a common-law privilege, were usually required by decisions of the U.S. Supreme Court. The plan for reapportionment of the Idaho legislature during the 1980s that had been adopted by the legislature had a population deviation of 33 percent between the smallest and the largest legislative district. The legislature had adopted this plan, although ten alternative plans had been offered that had deviation of less than 10 percent. The U.S. Supreme Court had held that a deviation in excess of 10 percent would require the state to offer a "satisfactory explanation."[27] The Idaho court declared the legislatively adopted plan unconstitutional.[28] The Idaho court concluded that the State had not made a "satisfactory explanation" of the 33 percent deviation, particularly in light of the number of reapportionment plans that had been offered that had acceptable deviation.

The Idaho court followed the dictates of the U.S. Supreme Court in four other case in which it invalidated laws passed by the Idaho legislature. Idaho law had provided for awards of alimony only to wives and not to husbands in divorce actions.[29] The U.S. Supreme Court had declared that a state law that provided for alimony only for wives violated the Equal Protection Clause of the Fourteenth Amendment of the U.S. Constitution.[30] As required by the clear command of the U.S. Supreme Court's decision, the Idaho court declared Idaho's alimony statute unconstitutional.[31] In two cases the U.S. Supreme Court had held that a state law that allowed a successful creditor in a small claims action to collect on the small claims judgment before the debtor could appeal was unconstitutional as a violation of the debtor's right of due process.[32] The Idaho court applied the U.S. Supreme Court decisions and declared that a part of the Idaho Small Claims Act that allowed a successful creditor to take the debtor's property before the appeal period had expired was unconstitutional.[33] The Idaho court held that the First Amendment to the U.S. Constitution required that a qualified privilege exists for newsmen to refuse to disclose their sources in a criminal trial. The Court first reviewed U.S. Supreme Court[34] and lower federal and state court decisions and concluded that "there was an increasing recognition by federal and state courts . . . that careful balancing by the courts between First Amendment privilege and any (conflicting) interest" is appropriate.[35] The Idaho court had earlier established the Idaho law of permissible police searches of automobiles without search warrants[36] in response to a U.S. Supreme Court decision. When the U.S. Supreme Court changed its position on the question, discrediting its earlier case on which the Idaho court had relied to establish the Idaho law, the Idaho court overruled its earlier cases to bring Idaho law into line with the current position of the U.S. Supreme Court.[37]

The traditional common law, which was reflected in the Idaho common law, required that the testimony of the complaining witness of a criminal rape be corroborated. When the Idaho court was first asked to abrogate this doctrine in 1980,[38] it refused; when it did finally change the rule, it changed it only prospectively, sending the immediate case back to the trial court to dismiss the rape charge because the complaining witnesses' testimony had not been corroborated.[39] Idaho was the next to the last state to abrogate the corroboration requirement.[40]

During the 1980s the Idaho court did recognize two new common-law causes of action, but that recognition was not enthusiastic. In a case of first impression for the court, it approved a restricted common-law cause of action against a certified accountant who negligently performed an audit. The court limited the availability of this cause of action to those the accountant *knew* would rely on the audit report.[41] The court refused to adopt the broader rule of the *Restatement (Second) of Torts*[42] that would have allowed anyone who relied on an audit report, whether or not the prospective reliance was known to the auditor, to sue for injury caused by the auditor's negligence. When asked to recognize the new causes of action of "wrongful birth" and "wrongful life"[43] against a negligent physician, the Idaho court recognized that the parents of a deformed infant had a cause of action against the negligent physician for "wrongful birth," but refused to recognize the deformed infant's cause of action for "wrongful life."[44]

FLORIDA

Florida Supreme Court Preferred Judicial Role

There was greater extra-judicial writing among the Florida judges than among the judges of many other courts, but there is nothing in this writing that directly answers the question of the judge's judicial role preferences. However, indirectly, the judges have given us glimpses that leaves their preferences in little doubt. Justice Grimes clearly assumed a restrained role when he wrote: "In the interest of predictability and stare decisis, the legal position of the court should not be changed every time a new justice comes on board. It is my belief that the court should proceed cautiously. . . . As a consequence I have already (in his second year on the court) voted in several cases contrary to my personal view of what might be a better rule."[45] Justice Overton approvingly quoted Alexander Hamilton in support of his position that "the judge must apply the law as written by the legislature . . . not as he or she might like the law to be": "'It can be no weight to say that the courts, on the pretense of repugnancy, may substitute their own pleasure to the constitutional intention of the legislature.'"[46] Justice England recognized that a 1980 amendment of the Florida Constitution that reduced the number of mandatory appeals the Florida court was required to hear and decide "provided the opportunity for . . . the justices of the Supreme Court to redefine the (court's) role" and "free the court from nonpolicy types of decisions, and direct its efforts to issues of statewide importance."[47] The justice took a look at this supposedly liberating constitutional amendment a year later and concluded that it had resulted in *no* change in the level of the court's policy making.[48]

The Florida Supreme Court during the 1970s had been relatively activist, rarely waiting for the legislature to solve the problems of society that became apparent through the cases on its docket, even those problems that seemed to result from legislative action. The court's attitude changed substantially with respect to societal problem solving as the 1980s began. The opinions of the 1980s Florida court are replete with appeals to the legislature to establish missing public policy. The best source of evidence of the judge's preferred judicial role, activist or restrained, is the opinions that they wrote when explaining the court's decisions. The judges referred problems to the legislature that arose from the application of common-law doctrine, from demands for the creation of new common-law causes of action, and from the application of legislative policy. Rosemary Burkett was the Florida court's first female justice and was thought by some to be a political activist. Her description of her preferred judicial role when the court, in a significant Florida case, refused to create a cause of action against a social host for the acts of an intoxicated guest exemplifies the choice of the court's justices: "Were I writing on a clean slate . . . I would agree that common-law principles of negligence are applicable to establish such liability. Since the legislature has acted . . . we cannot find social hosts more liable than the legislature has determined."[49]

Florida Court System

The structure of the Florida court system remained unchanged during the 1980s. The system was three-tiered, intermediate courts of appeal having been added in 1972.[50] The Florida court had seven judges,[51] who were appointed by the governor pursuant to a merit system of selection, and who served for six-year terms.[52] The court's chief justice was selected for a two-year term by the justices.[53]

Florida Supreme Court Cases, 1980–1990

The 1980s was a period of restrained decision making for the Florida Supreme Court. The court drew back from the relative activism of the preceding decade. The court refused to modify the existing Florida common-law doctrines that made it difficult or impossible for injured Florida residents to sue wrongdoers. When the court was asked to recognize a new cause of action, it routinely concluded that the legislature was the proper branch to establish the policy that would underlie a new right. In an unusual decision the court declared constitutional a legislatively prescribed statute of limitation that it had declared unconstitutional five years earlier with the effect of denying a person injured by a defective product the right to sue the manufacturer for injuries unless the injuries occurred *before the product was purchased*! In the court's only significant activist decision of the period, the court clearly preferred that the legislature would step in to decide the applicable Florida public policy.

Modification of the Common Law. During the 1980s many cases were taken to the Florida court by frustrated Florida plaintiffs who asked the court to modify many of the common-law doctrines that denied them a right to use the courts to seek redress for their injuries or that made their legal action substantially more difficult and their recovery less than complete. The Florida court was not a receptive bench. It left intrafamily tort immunity where it had been established by traditional predecessor courts. When it was asked to abrogate parent's common-law immunity from suits by their children, the court refused to eliminate the basic doctrine, but appeared to modify it by waiving the immunity "to the extent . . . of available insurance coverage."[54] However, the court took away what it appeared to have given. It affirmed that an exclusion in an automobile insurance policy for family members would be valid, an invitation that liability insurance companies would be unlikely to resist and that made the apparent amelioration of the doctrine largely illusory. Similarly, the court affirmed the continued vitality of the common-law interspousal immunity. The court held that the doctrine prevented a wife from suing her deceased husband's estate for injuries caused by the husband while alive.[55] This was a clear example of the court ignoring policy considerations and blindly following traditional doctrine: the underlying reason for the intrafamily immunities is that suits between family members would disrupt the harmony of the family and lead to family dissension, a result that could hardly result from a suit against a dead spouse's estate. Although the court had modified the parent-child immunity doctrine to the extent of available insurance coverage, it inexplicably refused to modify the interspousal immunity in a case where there was insurance coverage and concluded that even when insurance is available, suits of "spouse versus spouse have a potential disruptive effect on the marital unit,"[56] It offered no explanation of the difference in disruption between parent-child suits and husband-wife suits.

Until 1973, Florida law was controlled by the traditional sovereign immunity doctrine. In that year the Florida legislature by statute waived sovereign immunity for the state and its subdivisions.[57] The waiver, on its face, appeared to be absolute, but the Florida court limited the legislative waiver by interpreting the law to contain an exception for government "planning" activities.[58] In 1982, the court decided three cases in which it expanded the protection of governments for their planning activity to include protection from liability for the government's failure to install traffic lights at a dangerous intersection;[59] a failure to give drivers warning of a dangerous curve in a state road;[60] and a failure to protect an open waterway on city property.[61] In a later case the court interpreted the planning exception to include a failure by city police to impound a dog that was running loose after it had bitten people.[62] A law review writer concluded that "the court's departure from previous holdings had made sovereign immunity the rule rather than the exception."[63] In a decision in which it inexplicably held that the legislative waiver of sovereign immunity did not include negligent acts of firemen, the Florida court abdicated responsibility to interpret the statutory waiver and said that "if there is to be . . . liability of a governmental entity . . . for the action of fire-fighters . . . that duty must be established by an enactment of the legislature and not by judicial fiat."[64]

When the legislature passed laws to control the skyrocketing jury verdicts, the court routinely approved the legislative efforts to limit the amount an injured person could recover, although progressive state courts had found such limits to be invalid. The Florida legislature had limited the amount of recovery from the state or other governmental unit available in a personal injury case to $100,000.[65] The court approved the validity of this limitation, although a plaintiff, whose jury award of $150,000 had been reduced as a result of the legislative limitation, argued that the law violated her federal right of due process and her right of access to the courts, guaranteed by the Florida Constitution.[66] The legislature had also adopted a "no fault insurance law," a law protecting personal injury defendants generally. The law established a threshold that an injured person must meet in order to successfully maintain an action in court for injuries resulting from an automobile accident. This threshold eliminated an injured person's right to maintain an action for pain and suffering caused by another's negligence unless the pain and suffering had been accompanied by permanent injury or death.[67] A Florida tort law expert described this law as having "the most restrictive tort threshold of any no-fault act in the United States."[68] The Florida court affirmed the no fault law's constitutionality in a case in which a child had experienced substantial pain and suffering as a result of an automobile driver's negligence but suffered no permanent injuries, although the child's representative argued that the law denied him access to the courts in violation of the Florida Constitution and violated his federal constitutional rights of due process and equal protection.[69]

Although the trend in the states has been away from a negligence (fault) based test and toward a no-fault standard for tort liability, the Florida court affirmed the negligence (fault) test for Florida: "absent some fault on its part, an employer is not liable for punitive damages for the willful and wanton misconduct of its employees" when an employee causes injury.[70] The court reviewed a case in which a drunken employee truck driver killed the plaintiff's husband, for which a jury had given the wife $250,000 in punitive damages. The court "strict vicarious liability and moved in the direction of liability that is purely fault based."[71]

Joint and several liability is a doctrine of the traditional common-law that requires that any one of a number of persons who have jointly caused an injury may be held liable for the full amount of the resulting damage. This doctrine is inconsistent with the concept of comparative negligence, which is founded on the principle that each wrongdoer should be required to be responsible for injury to the extent of his/her fault. The Florida court, in the more activist decade of the 1970s, had established comparative negligence in Florida by its decision.[72] However, the 1980s court refused to abrogate the doctrine of joint and several liability in a case in which the jury had found Walt Disney World Co. to be one percent at fault, another defendant to be 85 percent at fault, and the plaintiff to be 15 percent at fault in causing the plaintiff's injury. The application of joint and several liability in this case required Walt Disney World Co. to pay the plaintiff 86 percent of her damages when she proceeded to collect, not surprisingly, against Disney and not the other wrongdoer. Although the court had earlier established comparative negligence in Florida by its decision and "while recognizing the logic of Disney's position," the "court believ(ed) that the viability of the doctrine (of joint and several liability) is a matter which should best be decided by the legislature."[73]

The court was equally hesitant to approve any deviation from the status quo when it was asked to eliminate meaningless, technical restrictions that disqualified persons from using the courts to redress injury. A Florida statute required that before a case is "instituted on a claim against the state or one of its agencies or subdivisions" "the claimant (must) present the claim in writing."[74] The Florida court threw out a suit against a hospital by the parents of a child who allegedly contracted meningitis as the result of a state hospital's negligence because the parents had not given the required notice in writing even though the hospital had actual notice of their claim.[75] The court similarly had allowed an insurance company to avoid its liability to a policy holder who had failed to give the insurance company notice of an accident within the time specified in a policy, although this technical defect had not caused the insurance company any prejudice.[76]

New Causes of Action. The court was unwilling to make public policy by recognizing new common-law causes of action. When injured plaintiffs asked it to approve new causes of action, the court routinely recognized the primacy of the legislature. In a case in which a father had been injured in an automobile accident that had left his children without his care, companionship, and guidance, the court refused to recognize that the children had a cause of action for loss of parental consortium against the negligent driver who had caused their father's injury.[77] The court concluded that "if the action is to be created, it is wiser to leave it to the legislative branch."[78] The court refused to recognize a cause of action against parents for lack of parental supervision of a child, whom his parents knew "roughly pushed and hit smaller children," when the unruly child caused $135,000 damage to a younger and smaller child with whom his parents had allowed him to play.[79]

As our society has become more complex, it has been increasingly difficult to know the specific cause of an injury. This is particularly true when the product that causes an injury is one of a number of very similar products produced by a number of different manufacturers and not differentiated in their use. Examples of such confusion are the administration of drugs in a hospital or by a physician to a patient and the exposure to building products that contain dangerous substances such as asbestos. "Market shares theory"[80] was developed and approved[81] to make the courts more available to one injured as a result of another's action by alleviating the difficulty in identifying the wrongdoer and making it easier to describe the cause of the injury in these circumstances. The Florida court refused to approve "market shares theory" because, although the plaintiff could not identify all the similar products he had encountered, he was able to "identify several."[82]

In 1987 and 1988, the Florida court refused the opportunity to create two new causes of action for injured Floridians. Characteristically, in both cases the court identified the Florida legislature as the appropriate policy maker. The Florida court was presented with one of the endemic social host cases. The court refused to recognize the responsibility of the social host for the acts of an intoxicated guest in a suit by a person who had been injured in an automobile accident caused by a minor who had been served alcoholic beverages at a party.[83] The court admitted that "such a cause of action may be socially desirable," but concluded that "the more prudent course is for this Court to defer to the legislative branch."[84] When the court was asked to approve the application of the "negligent entrustment doctrine"[85] to an automobile dealer who had sold and entrusted an automobile to a driver the dealer knew was an incompetent driver and who "shortly after leaving the dealership" was in an automobile accident, the court refused, stating that "of the three branches of government, the judiciary is the least capable of . . . resolving broad policy questions."[86]

In 1985, the Florida court took the unusual step of "receding" from an earlier decision in which it had declared unconstitutional a law passed by the legislature, resulting in that law becoming constitutional.[87] Florida law required that a cause of action against a manufacturer for injury caused by a defective product be begun within twelve years after the manufacturer sold the product, regardless of when the injury occurred.[88] This law effectively required a person to file an action for an *injury before the injury occurred* if it occurred more than twelve years after the product had been sold. An earlier court had declared that this law violated the Florida Constitution because it denied an injured person access to the courts. The court's 1985 decision that resurrected the law was doubly restrained: the court refused to hold an act of the legislature unconstitutional and effectively denied numerous injured Floridians a chance to seek relief for their injuries.

Criminal Law. The Florida court made restrained decisions in two criminal-related cases. A Florida law allowed the state to imprison parents who are delinquent in making child support payments.[89] In a case in which a delinquent parent challenged that the law violated the Florida Constitutions guarantee against imprisonment for debt,[90] the court held that the writers of the Constitution had used "debt" "in a broad sense" and, in this "broad sense," criminal imprisonment for debt did not violate the constitutional guarantee.[91] The traditional common-law test of mental capacity to commit a crime was the standard of the M'Naghten rule, which requires a person who knows the difference between right and wrong to be criminally responsible. Traditional courts do not allow a defendant to introduce evidence of his/her mental capacity that does not relate to this standard. Beginning in the 1950s, progressive courts began to allow defendants to offer evidence that they had "diminished capacity" at the time of a crime's commission for the purpose of proving that they did not have the intent that is an essential element of some crimes. When the Florida court was asked to approve a defense of diminished capacity offered by a defendant whose "intelligence was in the lowest five percent of the population," who had been "kicked in the head by a bull . . . which caused posttraumatic seizure disorder," and who had a passive personality that made him "easily led and manipulated," the Florida court refused to follow the lead of "approximately one-half the states and federal jurisdiction (that) now approve the (diminished capacity) defense." The court noted that "if such principles are to be incorporated into our law . . . the change should lie within the province of the legislature."[92]

PENNSYLVANIA

During the 1980s, the Pennsylvania Supreme Court was a deeply divided court. The division was not over the propriety of judicial policy making. The justices were occupied with personal, political, and professional animosities.[93] "Power grabs," and "personal dislikes" characterized the court during the decade. "Claims of power grabs and politics might sound absurd for most state supreme courts, they (were) routine for Pennsylvania's fractious high court."[94] There was convincing evidence of judicial irregularities in the court's official business. A prominent Pennsylvania newspaper, the Philadelphia *Inquirer*, questioned the propriety of certain campaign contributions accepted by three of the court's justices. "At least three members of the court" had received questionable campaign contributions while the court was considering a case from a contributor who was interested in the case's outcome and these contributions "may have . . . influenced" the court's decision.[95] These interpersonal hostilities and suspect judicial behavior blossomed into reciprocal charges of unethical behavior by two of the justices against each other, which led, in the next decade, to the impeachment of one of the justices.[96]

Pennsylvania Supreme Court Preferred Judicial Role

None of the 1980s judges of the Pennsylvania court has explained explicitly whether he or she believes that a high court should actively make public policy by its decision making. However, when the Pennsylvania judges' extra-judicial writing suggested a preference, it was for the traditional restrained judicial role. At a judicial orientation seminar, Justice Roberts quoted U.S. Supreme Court Justice Sutherland's description of the judicial function as "the essentially disinterested, rational and deliberate element of our democracy."[97] He described judicial restraint when he described good appellate judging: "A good judge respects and defends the separation of powers. He does not intrude into the provinces of the other coequal branches of government."[98]

Justice Hutchison described a restrained role for the judges when he sought to harmonize the common-law tradition with a statutory framework: "we should restrain ourselves from imposing our own personal views and solutions on the problems that come before us. Judges in America are not philosopher-kings, indebted to Plato, but are part of representative democracy that draws its rationale from Montesquieu."[99] In their decisions the justices frequently affirmed legislative policy, although questioning its wisdom, and looked to the legislature to correct problems that their cases had disclosed.

Pennsylvania Court System

There was no change in the structure of the Pennsylvania court system during the 1980s. The state's two intermediate courts of appeal[100] had been in place for some time. The Pennsylvania court had seven justices[101] who were initially elected in a partisan election and thereafter in retention elections[102] for ten-year terms.[103] The court's chief justice was the justice who had served on the court for the longest period.[104]

Pennsylvania Supreme Court Cases, 1980–1990

The Pennsylvania court in the 1980s was a much restrained state policy maker compared to the activist 1970s court that fully participated in state policy making. Strikingly, the 1973 court, by its decision, had abrogated the state's sovereign immunity. When the state legislature overruled the court's 1973 abrogation of the common-law doctrine and reestablished Pennsylvania's sovereign immunity by statute, the1980s Pennsylvania court supported the legislature's efforts at every opportunity. Repeatedly during the 1980s, when it was asked to approve a new cause of action to enable an injured person to sue for an injury, the Pennsylvania court asserted that creation of new causes of action was the function of the legislature. When the legislature did create a new right for individuals, the court consistently interpreted the legislature's acts narrowly for the protection of business interests.

Criminal Law. While the American courts, generally, were moving toward greater protection of the rights of those who were caught in the criminal justice system, the Pennsylvania court moved in the other direction. In 1976, the Pennsylvania court had appeared to move significantly away from the traditional M'Naghten rule,[105] the common-law test for criminal sanity, toward the more modern and progressive "irresistible impulse" rule.[106] This movement was halted in 1982 when the court was asked to approve the irresistible impulse test for criminal responsibility in a case in which the evidence supported the defendant's claim that he had been unable to control an urge to strangle his victim. The court affirmed that "(t)he M'Naghten test remains the law of Pennsylvania."[107] The court was not more considerate of defendants after their convictions. In 1986, the court considered a controversy that had been continuing for more than fourteen years with respect to the conditions in the Philadelphia municipal jails. One of the specific complaints was overcrowding of jail cells. Nine years earlier, the parties had agreed that Philadelphia's jail's population density would not exceed "one man, one cell" and a trial court had ordered the city to comply with its agreement. The

Pennsylvania court ignored the agreed "one man, one cell" standard and concluded that the trial court should use a "totality of the circumstances" evaluation to determine whether the triple-celled Philadelphia jails violated the Eighth Amendment "cruel and unusual punishment" prohibition.[108]

Workers' Compensation. The Pennsylvania court denied injured persons a cause of action in the courts for their injuries if the action would jeopardize the employer in any way or threaten the exclusivity of the workers' compensation process. The court's concern for the employer and the exclusivity of the process guaranteed complete immunity from suit if an employee was a party to the action in any capacity. When an employee sued a third party who had injured the employee while the employee was working and the *third party* was required to bring the employer into the suit to determine if the employer had any responsibility for the injury, the court denied the unrelated defendant the right, even though no claim was made against the employer.[109] In another workers' compensation case the employee had been injured while cutting up chickens with a "chicken saw" that had been manufactured by her employer. The "chicken saw" had been defectively manufactured and had caused the employee's injury. The injured employee sued her employer, alleging that the employer had a "dual capacity": as her employer in the chicken cutting duties and as a manufacturer in the operation of the saw. The Pennsylvania court rejected the "dual capacity" that had been recognized by the courts in other states[110] and denied the employee the right to maintain her action, although the court expressed concern that injury from "'Rube Goldberg' devices that put production above life and limb" should be "actionable beyond the limits of workmen's compensation."[111]

The Common Law. The court refused to disturb either commercial or criminal common-law doctrine that previous Pennsylvania courts had established. Earlier traditional courts had established the rule that in order to successfully maintain an action against a professional for malpractice, the injured person had to be "in privity"[112] with the professional. New Jersey law disqualified a person who had acted as a witness to a will from being either a beneficiary or executor of that will. A Pennsylvania lawyer, apparently in ignorance of this restriction, wrote a will for a New Jersey resident and allowed the person who was named as both the executor and the principal beneficiary of a will to act as a witness to that will. After a New Jersey court had disqualified the witness-executor-beneficiary, she sued the lawyer, charging that she had been injured as a result of this negligent malpractice. The witness-executor-beneficiary was not "in privity" with the lawyer and the Pennsylvania court affirmed the traditional privity doctrine of the Pennsylvania common-law, denying the injured witness-executor-beneficiary the right to sue the lawyer for his malpractice.[113] The traditional criminal common-law did not recognize the "battered woman syndrome"[114] as a defense to a criminal murder charge and the Court refused to disturb the established Pennsylvania common-law in this respect,[115] although a change had been forcefully advocated by "various organizations that provide services to the victims of domestic violence" in a brief they filed in the case as *amicus curiae.*[116]

The Pennsylvania court had abrogated the common-law doctrine of sovereign immunity by its decision in 1973.[117] In response, the Pennsylvania legislature passed laws selectively reestablishing Pennsylvania's governments protection from lawsuits. One of these laws, the Political Subdivision Tort Claims Act,[118] provided immunity for Pennsylvania's subdivisions for "almost all tort liability."[119] A mother attempted to sue a county for the wrongful death of her son who had committed suicide while he was in the custody of the county. The county had failed to supervise his custody, although it had knowledge that he was depressed and had previously attempted to commit suicide. The mother challenged the constitutionality of the immunity that the Political Subdivision Tort Claims Act gave to the county as a violation of the Pennsylvania Constitution's guarantee that "(a)ll courts shall be open, and every man for an injury done him shall have remedy by due course of law."[120] The Pennsylvania court denied the mother's right to maintain the suit and affirmed the legislature's reestablishment of the subdivision's sovereign immunity, observing that "(i)t is not our function to displace a rationally based legislative judgment."[121] "The turbulent history of governmental imunity is reflected in the *Carroll* court's willingness to reject past judicial interpretation and initiative in favor of deference to the legislature."[122] Another provision of the Political Subdivision Tort Claims Act limited the total possible liability of a subdivision to $500,000 for each negligent act. The city of Philadelphia had been responsible for a gas explosion that had killed seven people, injured many others, and caused extensive property damage. In all, seventy-two claims were filed against the City for injuries resulting from the explosion, far exceeding the $500,000 limitation. The Pennsylvania court rejected a claim that the limitation of total liability to $500,000 was unconstitutional,[123] although other state courts were invalidating their legislature's attempts to limit the amount an injured person could recover from a wrongdoer.[124]

New Causes of Action. The Pennsylvania court was not sympathetic to injured Pennsylvania plaintiffs when they sought its approval of new causes of action. The ubiquitous 1980s question of the liability of social hosts for the acts of their guests was presented to the court in two cases that were argued to the Pennsylvania court on the same day in 1983. The court answered them differently depending on the policy the legislature preferred. In the first case, a guest, who was visibly intoxicated, had been served alcoholic beverages by his host who knew that the guest would be driving an automobile. Later, the intoxicated guest caused an automobile accident that resulted in the death of one person and the injury of others. The court denied those injured and representative of the person killed the right to maintain an action against the intoxicated driver's host. The court based its decisions in the common-law doctrine that it is the consumption of alcohol rather than serving it that causes accidents.[125] In the second case, a minor had attended his employer's Christmas party and had been served alcoholic beverages. Although the employer's agents knew the minor was intoxicated, he was given the keys to his automobile. While driving home from the party, the minor caused an accident in which he was injured and he sued his employer for his injuries. The Pennsylvania court, in this second case, considered a law passed by the Pennsylvania legislature[126] that it found contained legislative policy that "persons under twenty-one years of age are incompetent to handle alcohol" and that "both minors and the public at large are to be protected from . . . serving alcohol to persons under twenty-one years of age."[127] In this second case the court rejected the common-law doctrine that consumption rather than serving causes injury and accepted the legislature's policy that minor drinkers should be protected from the consequences of being served alcoholic beverages and approved the minor's cause of action based on the liability of a social host for his guest's acts.[128]

At a time when progressive state courts were recognizing the contribution a spouse makes to the attainment of a professional degree by identifying such degree as marital property in the event of divorce, the Pennsylvania court refused to allow a wife who had supported her husband and family, including three minor children, and "facilitated" her husband's medical education, to claim a share in the value of her husband's medical degree. It based its decision on the traditional definition of property, and concluded that a professional degree was not "property" that could be divided between the spouses in the event of divorce.[129] In another case in which the Pennsylvania court refused to follow a progressive trend in the law, it refused to approve a claim against an insurance company for the company's bad faith refusal to settle an insurance claim. The court concluded that "it is for the Legislature to announce and implement the Commonwealth's policy governing the regulation of insurance carriers,"[130] and denied a property insurance policy holder the right to sue his insurance carrier for bad faith in refusing to pay a claim and then refusing to give the insured any information that would support the company's denial.[131]

The Pennsylvania court reached the same decisions that the Idaho and West Virginia courts did when it was asked to approve the related new causes of action of "wrongful birth" and "wrongful life." In the Pennsylvania case a physician negligently performed a sterilization procedure on a man who had a genetic defect that caused his children to be born with an incurable disease. After the attempted sterilization and after the physician had assured him that he was sterile, the man fathered a child who had the incurable disease. In two cases that the Pennsylvania court decided together, the parents had sued the negligent physician who had failed to sterilize the father for the "wrongful birth" of their child and, on behalf of the affected child, for "wrongful life." The court affirmed the parent's cause of action for "wrongful birth" for their expenses of the birth and raising of the affected child, but rejected the cause of action on behalf of the child for "wrongful life."[132]

The Pennsylvania court refused to approve a cause of action for tenants against their landlords when their landlord failed to exercise reasonable care to protect the tenant from criminal acts on the landlord's premises. Two tenants of a large apartment complex had been subjected to criminal activity that the court described as "a terrible penalty for their defenseless innocence." There had been twenty-one separate instances of criminal conduct in the apartment complex within the prior three-month period. When the tenants sued the landlord, the Pennsylvania court affirmed the traditional common-law rule that landlords do not have a duty to protect their tenants from criminal acts.[133] This affirmation of the traditional common-law doctrine drew harsh criticism in a Pennsylvania law review: "The *Feld* court indicated that it did not wish to follow the modern trend of imposing on landlords a duty to provide some type of security for their tenants."[134] "In recent years . . . courts have relied on a variety of theories to bring down the legal barrier that for centuries has shielded landlords from such liability."[135] "The court took a step backward in *Feld* and left tenants of urban multiple unit dwellings unnecessarily vulnerable to criminal assault"[136]

A political party attempted to rely on the Pennsylvania Constitution's guarantees of the right of free speech and petition[137] to establish its right to engage in political activity in a shopping mall. The California court had decided that the California Constitution supported this right to engage in political activity in a shopping center. In deciding the Pennsylvania case, the Pennsylvania court recognized that the relevant provisions of the California Constitution "are substantially the same as our own," and that the facts of the California case "are almost identical to this case."[138] Before the Pennsylvania court ruled, the supreme courts in Massachusetts,[139] Washington[140] and New Jersey[141] had followed the progressive California decision. Nevertheless, the Pennsylvania court denied the political party the right to maintain an action against the mall's owner for access to the mall.[142]

NOTES

1. The Hon. Robert E. Bakes, "The First Amendment-Second to None in the Constitution," *Advocate* (Idaho) 31 (October, 1988): 12.

2. Chapter 150, Sections 1–31, 1971 Idaho Sessions Law 743.

3. The Hon. Robert C. Huntley, Jr., "Sovereign Immunity and Reemergence of the Governmental/Proprietary Distinction: A Setback in Idaho's Governmental Liability Law," *Idaho Law Review* 20 (Spring, 1984): 197–241.

4. The Hon. Charles R. Donaldson, "Chief Justice's State of the Judiciary Address to the Idaho Bar Association Annual Meeting," *Advocate* (Idaho) 23: 1.

5. The Hon Byron Johnson, AIn Memoriam: Justice Allen G. Shepard 1922–1989" 26 *Idaho Law Review* (No.1, 1989-1990) 1–5, at p. 2.

6. The Hon. Robert E. Bakes, AIn Memoriam: Justice Allen G. Shepard 1922–1989" 26 *Idaho Law Review* (No.1, 1989–1990) 5–7, at p. 6.

7. Idaho Code Section 1-201.

8. 1-5 Idaho Code Section 1-2-1.

9. Idaho Code Section 34-905.

10. Idaho Code Section 1-201.

11. *Book of the States 1988–89*, "State Courts of Last Resort (Table 4.1)" (Lexington, Ky.: The Council of State Governments), p. 157.

12. Idaho Code Section 41-2502.

13. *Nationwide Insurance Company v. Scarlett*, 788 P.2d 1317 (1989),

dissent of Justice Bistline at p. 1318.

14. Underinsured motorists are motorists who cause damage that exceeds the limits of their insurance protection and leave their victims unable to recover the full amount of the minimum liability coverage required of all Idaho drivers.

15. *Blackburn v. State Farm Mutual, etc.*, 697 P.2d 425 (1985).

16. *Meckert v. Transamerica Insurance Company*, 701 P.2d 217 (1985), at p. 220.

17. *Dullenty v. Rocky Mountain Fire and Casualty Company*, 721 P.2d 198 (1986).

18. *Hammon v. Farmer's Insurance Company of Idaho*, 707 P.2d 397 (1985).

19. *Hammon*, at p. 401.

20. *Huyuck v. Heckla Mining Company*, 612 P.2d 142 (1980); see, generally, "Modern Status of Rules Conditioning Landowner's Liability Upon Status of Injured Party as Invitee, licensee, or Trespasser," 32 ALR 3d 508.

21. *Tusch v. Coffin*, 740 P.2d 1022 (1987).

22. *Hathaway v. Krumery*, 716 P.2d 1287 (1986).

23. *Gamble v. Kinch*, 629 P.2d 1168 (1981).

24. Idaho Code Section 45-701.

25. *Merritt v. The State of Idaho*, 742 P.2d 397 (1986).

26. *Merritt*, at p. 402.

27. *Brown v. Thompson*, 462 U.S. 835 (1983).

28. *Hellar, et al. v. Cenarrusa, et al.*, 682 P.2d 539 (1984).

29. Idaho Code Section 32-706.

30. *Orr v. Orr*, 440 U.S. 268 (1979).

31. *Murphey v. Murphey*, 653 P.2d 441 (1982).

32. *Sniadach v. Family Finance Corp.*, 395 U.S.337 (1969) and *Fuentes v. Shevin*, 407 U.S. 17 (1972).

33. *Frizzell v. Swoford*, 663 P.2d 1125; the parts of the Idaho Small Claims Act that the Court declared unconstitutional were Idaho Code Sections 1-2311 and 1-2312.

34. *Branzburg v. Hayes*, 408 U.S. 665 (1972). The Court relied heavily on the concurring opinion of Justice Powell that advanced a balancing test to determine when the First Amendment required that a privilege exists. Justice Powell was the necessary fifth justice in the Supreme Court's 5–4 majority.

35. *Contempt of Jim Wright*, 700 P.2d 40 (1985).

36. *State v. Miles*, 545 P.2d 484 (1976) and *State v. Post*, 573 P.2d 153 (1978).

37. *State v. Bottleson*, 625 P.2d 1093 (1981).

38. *State v. Tisdell*, 607 P.2d 1326 (1980).

39. *State v. Byers*, 627 P.2d 788 (1981).

40. After Idaho, only Nebraska required corroboration.

41. *Idaho Bank & Trust Co. v. First Bancorp of Idaho*, 772 P.2d 720 (1989)

42. Section 552.

43. See Chapter 3, Notes 19 and 20.

44. *Blake v. Cruz*, 698 P.2d 315 (1984).

45. The Hon. Stephen H. Grimes, "From DCA Judge to Justice: Subtle Differences," *Florida Bar Journal* 62 (May, 1988): 20–21.

46. The Hon. Ben F. Overton, "Trial Judges and Political Elections: A Time for Re-Examination," *University of Florida Journal of Law and Public Policy* 2 (1989): 9.

47. The Hon. Arthur J. England, Jr., Eleanor Mitchell Hunter, and Richard C. Williams, Jr., "An Analysis of the 1980 Jurisdictional Amendment," *Florida Bar Journal* 54 (June 1980): 406.

48. The Hon. Arthur J. England, Jr. and Richard C. Williams, Jr., "Florida Appellate Reform: One Year Later," *Florida Bar Journal* 55 (Nov. 8, 1981):704–712.

49. *Bankston v. Brennen*, 507 So.2d 1385 (1987), at pp 1387–1388.

50. Constitution of the State of Florida, Article V, Section 4.

51. Constitution of the State of Florida, Article V, Section 3.

52. Constitution of the State of Florida, Article V, Section 11.

53. *Book of the States, 1988-1989*, "State Courts of Last Resort (Table 4.1)" (Lexington, Ky.: The Council of State Governments), p. 157.

54. *Ard v. Ard*, 414 So.2d 1066 (1982).

55. *Hill v. Hill*, 415 So.2d 20 (1982).

56. *Snowten v. United States Fidelity and Guaranty Company*, 475 So.2d 1211 (1985).

57. Florida Statute, Section 768.28 (1983).

58. *Commercial Carrier Corp. v. Indian River County*, 371 So.2d 1010 (1979).

59. *Department of Transportation v. Neilson, et al.*, 419 So.2d 1071 (1982). Failure to install a traffic light is planning?

60. *Ingham v. State*, 419 So.2d 1081 (1982). Failure to give a warning is planning?

61. *City of St. Petersburg v. Collom*, 419 So.2d 1082 (1982).

62. *Carter, etc. v. City of Stuart, et al.*, 468 So.2d 955 (1985). A dog at loose is planning?

63. Student note, "Rebuilding the Wall of Sovereign Immunity: Municipal Liability for Negligent Building Inspection," *University of Florida Law Review* 37 (1986): 343, 371.

64. *City of Daytona Beach v. Palmer*, 469 So.2d 121 (1985).

65. Florida Statute, Section 768. 28(5) (1979).

66. *Cauley v. City of Jacksonville*, 403 So.2d 379 (1981).

67. Florida Statute, Section 627.737(2) (1979).

68. Marilyn Lipton, "Florida No-Fault: The Court Went Along for the Ride," *Stetson Law Review* 12 (1983): 836.

69. *Chapman, et al. v. Dillon, et al.*, 415 So.2d 12 (1982).

70. *Mercury Motors Express, Inc v. Smith*, 393 So.2d 545 (1981).

71. James C. Holiczer, "The Employer's Liability for Punitive damages for the Acts of an Employee," *Stetson Law Review* 11 (1982): 570, at p. 572.

72. *Hoffman v. Jones*, 280 So.2d 431 (1973).

73. *Walt Disney World Co., et al. v. Wood, et al.* 515 So. 2d 198 (1987), see, p. 202.

74. Florida Statute 768.28(6) (1977).

75. *Menendez v. North Broward Hospital District*, 537 So.2d 889 (1988).

76. *Banker's Insurance Company v. Macias*, 475 So.2d 1216 (1985).

77. Parental consortium as described by the court is parent's "care, comfort, society, companionship, instruction and guidance." *Zorzos, et al. v. Rosen, et al.*, 467 So.2d 305 (1985).

78. *Zorzos v. Rosen*, at p. 307.

79. *Snow v. Nelson*, 475 So.2d 225 (1985).

80. Market shares theory is common-law doctrine that can be utilized by those injured by the cumulative exposure to products of more than one manufacturer who do not know the identity of the manufacturer of the specific injurious product to join as defendants all the manufacturers of the product and that allows the court to apportion each manufacturer's liability according to its percentage of the market output. *Celotex Corporation, et al. v. Copeland, et al.*, 471 So.2d 533 (1985).

81. See *Sindell v. Abbot Laboratories*, 607 P.2d 924 (1980); Section 433 B(3), *Restatement(Second) of Torts* (1965)

82. *Celotex Corporation v. Copeland*.

83. *Bankston, et ux. v. Brennan, et al.*, 507 So.2d 1385 (1987).

84. *Bankston v. Brennen*, at p. 1387.

85. *Restatement(Second) of Torts*, Section 390 (1969).

86. *Horne v. Vic Potamkin Chevrolet, Inc.*, 533 So.2d 261 (1988).

87. *Pullom v. Cincinnati, Inc.*, 476 So.2d 657 (1985).

88. Florida Statute Section 95.031(2) (1979).

89. Florida Statute Section 409.2561(1)-(3) (1979), that provides, in part: "(1) Any payment of public assistance money made to any dependent child creates a *debt* . . . (3) . . . the recipient (of public assistance money) is deemed . . . to have appointed the department to . . . (4) Pursu(e) civil *and criminal* enforcement of support obligations." (Emphasis added.)

90. Article I, Section 11, Florida Constitution.

91. *Lamm v. Chapman*, 413 So.2d 749 (1982).

92. *Chestnut v. State of Florida*, 538 So.2d 820 (1989), quoting *Bethea v. United States*, 365 A.2d 64 (D.C. App. 1976), at p. 92.

93. *National Law Journal*, 5 (June 27, 1983): 1, 27, 28 & 32.

94. Joseph A. Slobodzian, "Infighting Rips Pa. High Court," *National Law Journal* 14 (December 14, 1992): 3.

95. *National Law Journal*, 5 (June 27, 1983): 1, at p. 28.

96. *American Bar Association Journal*, 70 (March, 1984): 38.

97. *Pennsylvania Bar Association Quarterly* 53(July, 1982): 167–171, at p. 169.

98. The Hon. Samuel J. Roberts, "What Makes a Good Appellate Judge," *Judges Journal* 22:15, at p. 51.

99. The Hon. William D. Hutchison, "Forward" to the "Pennsylvania Supreme Court Review, 1985," *Temple Law Quarterly* 59: 546, at p. 548.

100. 42 Pa. C.S. Section 705.

101. Pennsylvania Constitution, Article 5, Section. 2.

102. Pennsylvania Constitution, Article 5, Section 13.

103. Pennsylvania Constitution, Article 5, Section 15.

104. *Book of the States, 1988–1989*, "State Courts of Last Resort (Table 4.1)" (Lexington, Ky.: The Council of State Governments), p. 157.

105. The M'Naghten rule is a rule of criminal law that provides that one is sane and responsible for the criminal consequences of his/her act if he/she knows the difference between right and wrong and knows the nature and quality of the act.

106. *Commonwealth v. Walzack*, 360 A.2d 914 (1976). The "irresistible impulse" test for criminal responsibility excuses a defendant who is unable to resist a compulsion to act criminally even though he/she knew the difference between right and wrong.

107. *Commonwealth v. Weinstein*, 451 A.2d 1344 (1982).

108. *Jackson v. Hendrick*, 503 A.2d 400 (1986).

109. *Heckendorn v. Consolidated Rail Corporation, et al.*, 465 A.2d 609 (1983).

110. See "Pennsylvania Supreme Court Review" *Temple Law Review* 62, 1981: p. 795, n. 10.

111. *Heath v. Church's Fried Chicken, Inc., et al.*, 546 A.2d 1120.

112. "Privity" is a shared commercial relationship, such as lawyer-client, doctor-patient, which requires that the party that has been served pays the other for the service.

113. *Guy v. Liederbach, et al.*, 459 A.2d 744 (1983).

114. "A battered woman is a woman who is repeatedly subjected to any forceful physical or psychological behavior by a man in order to coerce her to do something he wants her to do without any concern for her rights." *Commonwealth v. Stonehouse*, 555 A.2d 772 (1989), at p. 783.

115. *Commonwealth v. Stonehouse.*

116. The Court did agree that evidence that a defendant was a battered woman could be admitted in a murder trial to demonstrate the defendant's fear in support of a claim of self defense.

117. *Ayala v. Philadelphia Board of Public Education*, 305 A.2d 877 (1973).

118. 42 Pa. C.S. Section 8541, et seq.

119. "Pennsylvania Supreme Court Review," *Temple Law Quarterly* 55, 1981: 622–885.

120. Article I, Section II, Pennsylvania Constitution.

121. *Carroll v. County of York*, 437 A.2d 394 (1981).

122. "Pennsylvania Supreme Court Review," *Temple Law Quarterly* 55, 1981:622-885, at p. 643.

123. *Smith v. City of Philadelphia*, 516 A.2d 306 (1986).

124. See, e.g., *Morris v. Savoy*, 576 N.E.2d (Ohio) 765 (1991).

125. *Klein v. Raisinger, et al.*, 470 A.2d 507 (1983).

126. Pa.C.S. Section 6308.

127. *Congini, etc, et al. v. Portersville Valve Company*, 470 A.2d 515 (1983), at p. 517 and 518.

128. *Congini v. Portersville.*

129. *Hodge v. Hodge*, 520 A.2d 15 (1986).

130. *D'Ambrosio v. Pennsylvania National Mutual Casualty Insurance Company*, 431 A.2d 966 (1981), at p. 970.

131. *D'Ambrosio v. Pennsylvania Mutual.*

132. *Speck, et al. v. Finegold, et al.*, 439 A.2d 110 (1981).

133. *Feld, et al. v. Merriam et al.*, 485 A.2d 742 (1984).

134. "The Foreseeability of Apartment Living: Pennsylvania Defines a Landlord's Duty to Provide Security," *Villanova Law Review* 31, 1986: 627, at p. 629.

135. "The Foreseeability of Apartment Living," at p.627.

136. "The Foreseeability of Apartment Living," at p. 666.

137. Article I, Section II, Pennsylvania Constitution.

138. *Western Pennsylvania Socialist Workers 1982 Campaign, et al v. Connecticut General Life Insurance Company*, 515 A.2d 1331 (1986), at p. 1338.

139. *Batchelder v. Allied Stores*, 445 N.E.2d 590.

140. *Alderwood Associates v. Washington Environmental Council*, 635 P.2d 108 (1981).

141. *State v. Schmid*, 423 A.2d 615 (1980).

142. *Western Pennsylvania Socialist Workers etc v. Connecticut etc..*

Chapter 6

Comparisons and Conclusions

The comparison of three state supreme courts that each had an activist advocate member and each of which was an intentional active policy maker in its state during the late 1970s or 1980s with three other courts that did not have an advocate judge and did not make policy for its state during the 1980s strongly suggests a significant relationship between activist advocacy and judicial policy making. The comparison of the policy making in the Indiana, West Virginia, and Ohio courts eliminates as possible explanations of the court's decisions to make policy a number of institutional and environmental characteristics of the courts that have some explanatory promise. Finally, the different purposes and goals of the activist advocacy of Justices Shepard, Neely, and Celebrezze leads to conclusions about the permanence of the resulting judicial policy making.

SIX-COURT COMPARISON

Chapters 2, 3, 4 and 5 present a comparison of state courts with an activist advocate that were policy makers with state courts without such an advocate that declined to make policy with their decisions. Each of the courts that had an activist advocate substituted their preferred policy for the state policy that their legislatures had established, abrogated the policy of the common law that their predecessor courts had established, and refused to recognize the superiority of their state's legislature as a policy maker.

The Ohio court overruled the state legislature's policy that workers would be confined to the workers' compensation system for compensation for work-related injuries.[1] The court substituted its preferred policy that opened the way for Ohio workers to participate in the bonanza of skyrocketing jury verdicts. The West Virginia court threw out the state's sovereign immunity, a policy that had been established by earlier courts. The court went so far as to suggest that it was prepared to overrule the West Virginia Constitution.[2] The Indiana court refused to recognize the primacy of legislative policy making. In a case in which the court decided not to change established state policy, it nevertheless firmly proclaimed that the inherent policy question was "entirely appropriate for judicial determination."[3]

The three restrained courts that were described in Chapter 5 regularly affirmed legislative policy and their state's common law and recognized their legislature as their state's prime policy maker. The Pennsylvania court refused to depart from the restrictive workers' compensation law that denied Pennsylvania workers the right to sue their employers in Pennsylvania courts, even though the court recognized that an injured worker had a cause that should be "actionable beyond the limits of Workmen's Compensation."[4] After the Florida legislature appeared to have waived the state's common-law protection of sovereign immunity, the Florida court reduced the extent of the waiver in successive cases. The court's contraction of the effect of the legislative abrogation made "sovereign immunity the rule rather than the exception."[5] Each of these states, characteristically, regularly appealed to the state legislature to change established policy with which they disagreed. The Idaho court refused to impose its preferred policy in cases dealing with the state's uninsured motorists coverage law, though it found the legislative policy to be inequitable and undesirable. The court "urge(d) legislative action."[6]

The six states whose courts were compared are dissimilar. They are located in five different regions of the country: the Midwest, the border, the West, the South and the East. Their economies have different bases: farming, industry, mining, and commerce. Their economic fortunes range from stable to erratic, being very responsive to every change in the economy. These differences in the states make it likely that the conclusions that we can reach as a result of their comparison are not related to local or peculiarly local influences. The states' dissimilarity reinforces the conclusions that courts whose judges included an activist advocate made policy in their states while the courts without an activist advocate were restrained in their decision making, allowing others to make their states' policy.

THREE-COURT COMPARISON

In Chapters 2, 3, and 4 we looked at the Indiana, West Virginia, and Ohio courts for approximately ten-year periods beginning on various dates in the late 1970s or early 1980s. Each of these courts had a period of active policy making and these chapters illuminated the level of activism that each of these courts manifested during their activist decade. In the Indiana court, the activist period directly followed a period that was virtually barren of activism. Similarly, in Ohio, the activism of the early 1980s followed an extended period of traditional decision making and the court's period of hyperactivism was followed by a period of lessened, though significant, activism. During the period 1977 to 1986, the West Virginia court increased the level of activism that had begun in 1973 and the level of activism was significantly high during the period. These surveys of the three courts revealed ten factors that could have influenced the court to become a policy maker. There were three potentially influential institutional factors: the degree of control a court had over its docket, the presence of an intermediate appellate court, and the use of an elective or merit system for the selection of its high court judges. Three environmental factors that were potentially influential were uncovered: the existence of political gridlock in the state's law-making machinery, the political party of the court's majority, and one-party domination of the court. Some of these factors were present during both a court's activist and non-activist, or less activist, periods. Significantly, none of these institutional and environmental factors was present in all of the three courts during their activist periods, although, in various combinations, some were present in each of the three courts. The three chapters did reveal that each court had an activist advocate during its activist period. Chapter 5 examined three state courts during comparable periods in which none had a judge who advocated judicial policy making. None of these courts was an activist decision maker nor a significant policy maker in its state during the period.[7]

A factor that had the same influence on a court during periods of both activism and non-activism or during both strong and less strong activist periods can not explain either the existence of a court's activism or its changed intensity. A constant influence cannot explain both the presence and absence of the same condition. Similarly, logically, the same factor cannot explain both why a court is highly activist and why the same court becomes less active. In these three 1980s courts, both the institutional and environmental factors that seem to promise an explanation of the court's choice of judicial activism are negated because their effect remained constant while the level of judicial activism varied.

Institutions

Intermediate Appellate Courts. The structural systems of the courts are among such potential explanatory factors that are disqualified by their constancy. The judicial system of Indiana was three-tiered during both the non-activist first half of the decade as well as during the activist second half. As in Indiana, the intermediate appellate court was in place in the Ohio system during the existence of traditional decision making (before 1980), during the active Celebrezze court, and during the subsequent, less active Moyer court. In West Virginia there was no intermediate appellate court and the court was an active policy maker during the entire period, but the West Virginia court system had not had intermediate courts prior to the 1970s when it was decidedly traditional in its decision making. The existence of the intermediate appellate cannot explain, by itself, the change to activism in Indiana and West Virginia, nor can it explain the reduced level of activism in Ohio. Each of the three courts that were examined in Chapter 5 that were not active policy makers was part of a system that had an intermediate appellate court. In combination with other factors, a state's court structure can perhaps contribute to an explanation of active decision making, but it is not a sufficient explanation standing alone.

There were two structural factors that determine a court's ability to control the cases it hears that demand further consideration: docket control and mandatory appeals.

Docket Control. The discretion that a court has to consider any case that is appealed to it is related to the degree of control that it has over its docket. The West Virginia court does not have to hear and decide any case that is attempted to be appealed to it; it has absolute control over its docket and it is unique in this respect among state supreme courts. The coincidence of the West Virginia court's extraordinary activism during the late 1970s and 1980s with its unique absolute discretion during this activist decade suggests that absolute docket control can explain that activism. While the West Virginia court's control is unique in its docket control, it is not the only state supreme court to have been activist; other courts that do not have the West Virginia court's control (e.g., Indiana's and Ohio's, specifically during the 1980s) did make policy decisions. Obviously, then, a court does not have to have total docket control to be active. Neither the Indiana nor Ohio court had unlimited docket control during the periods of their activism. Nor is complete docket discretion a sufficient cause of activism. Significantly, the West Virginia court had absolute control of its docket during the period antedating 1974 when it was without any claim to activist credentials. Here again, docket control in combination with other factors may contribute to a court's decision to be a policy maker, but it is not sufficient by itself to cause the activist decision making.

Mandatory Appeals. The forty-nine state high courts, other than West Virginia, are required, either by state law or constitution, to hear certain classes of cases. The necessity for Proposition 2 in Indiana emphasized the Indiana Constitutional requirement that the Indiana court had to consider most criminal appeals. In Indiana the scope of the mandatory criminal appeal was reduced by the passage of Proposition 2 during the period examined. Passage of Proposition 2 substantially increased the Indiana court's control of its docket and gave it more time to consider and devise new policy solutions for its pending cases. The reduced docket had the potential to increase that court's activism by freeing time and effort that would otherwise have been required of the court to decide mandatory criminal case appeals. However, the adoption of Proposition 2 cannot explain the rebirth of activism in the Indiana court. Proposition 2 did not become effective until three years after judicial activism was reborn. Furthermore, Proposition 2 only increased the court's discretion; it did not initiate it. The Ohio court was required to hear appeals from the State's Public Utilities Commission and the Board of Tax Appeals; these requirements existed during its most active policy-making period, 1980 to 1986, and this requirement did not prevent its policy making.

Selection Systems. The method by which the justices were selected in the three active policy-making courts, merit selection in Indiana and election in West Virginia and Ohio—continued unchanged during the entire decade. The merit system insulated the justices of the Indiana court during the 1980s from the necessity of running in a contested competitive elections in order to retain their seats. However, merit system appointment had also been used to select a majority of the members of that court who served in its previous non-activist period, 1980 to 1985; only two of the six incumbents during the court's activist period had initially ascended by election, and even these two had been insulated from the requirement of running in a contested election by the adoption of the merit system after their initial election and before the court's period of activism in the 1980s.

The decidedly different levels of active policy making in the Ohio court during the 1980's negates election systems as an explanation of judicial activism. If risk takers who are willing to engage successively in two contested elections to gain and retain a high court seat are more likely to be policy makers, that likelihood cannot explain court activism. Eleven of the thirteen Ohio justices who served during the decade of the 1980s and a majority of both the activist and non-activist Ohio courts had been initially selected in contested partisan nominating elections and nonpartisan, though contested, general elections. One justice who had initially been appointed[8] had been required to run in a contested judicial election in 1980, during the court's earlier traditional period, and the other appointed justice[9] had been on the court only briefly before her defeat in the general election of 1982. The same selection system that produced the early 1980s court with its intense activism also produced the late 1980s court that was significantly less active. The West Virginia judges who served both prior to and during the court's activist decision making during the 1980s were elected. Selection systems may contribute to the existence of activism in combination with other variables but cannot be sufficient of themselves.

Environment

Partisan Division. Similar to the structural factors, partisan division of the Indiana and Ohio courts remained constant during the decade, though with different balances. In Indiana, the court was split, with Republican justices being in the majority and the Democrats in the minority for the entire time. The Ohio court was also divided by party for the decade of the 1980s. Until January 1987, Democrats controlled the court and it had a Republican minority; during the succeeding four years Republicans had a majority and the Democrats were in the minority. If the dynamism that results from partisan political division can drive an appellate court to activism, it is, nevertheless, not sufficient by itself to explain the presence, absence, or level of activism of either the Indiana or Ohio court during the 1980s. Nor is it necessary. During the entire active period, from 1977 to 1987, the West Virginia court was made up exclusively of Democratic justices and the court's political unity coexisted with its active policy making.

One Party Control. The majority of the justices of the Indiana Supreme Court were Republicans during the non-activist early years of the 1980s as well as during the decade's later active years, which disqualifies Republican control as a sufficient prerequisite for activism. The inability of Republican control to explain judicial activism is affirmed by the activist behavior of the West Virginia court that had no Republican members during its decade of activism. Nor is exclusive Democratic tenure a satisfactory explanation. The Republican control of the Indiana court in the late 1980s, when activism in that court reached its modern zenith as well as the Republican majority on the post-1986 Ohio court, deny the necessity of Democratic control of the court in order that the court make policy.

Gridlock. Both the legislature and governor's office in West Virginia were controlled by the same political party, the Democratic, for the entire period of activism, 1977 to 1986, assuring that the legislative-executive law-making machinery was free of the partisan gridlock that could have created a policy vacuum.[10] Such a vacuum might increase the likelihood that the state's high court would feel it was necessary to step up and fill a policy-making void and, conversely, that in the absence of gridlock judicial policy making was unnecessary. Rather than decreasing the high court's policy involvement, the freedom of the other branches from gridlock coincided with high level of court activism, higher than in the immediately preceding period when there had been a Republican governor and a legislature controlled by the Democratic party. The shifting partisan strengths in Indiana and Ohio reinforce the conclusion that the absence of partisan legislative-executive gridlock does not deter a state's highest court from greater activism. In both Indiana and Ohio, the courts reached their highest level of activism during the years when both houses of the legislatures and the governors' offices were controlled by the same political party. Tables 6.1 and 6.2 show the relation of political gridlock to activist decision making in the Indiana and Ohio courts, respectively.

Ideology. Because of the prominence that ideology and policy preference have attained as the explanation of active judicial policy-making, a look at them from the perspective of our three policy making state courts is warranted. A court's ideology, its collective attitude, which may explain decision making in the U.S. Supreme Court, comes up short as an explanation of the decision making of the sister state courts. There was no change in the ideology of the Indiana court at the time of the advent of that court's activism in late 1985 and the court's constant ideological tenor necessarily negates ideology as a sufficient condition for the activism that the Indiana court manifested. The only change in the personnel of the court at about the time of the advent of activism was the replacement of Republican Justice Hunter, who had regularly joined Democrat DeBruler in registering activist dissents during his tenure on the court, by Republican Justice Shepard, who had a background of service in national and local Republican politics. The replacement of dissenting Republican Justice Hunter by Republican Justice Shepard should not have changed the ideological balance of the Indiana court. If it had any effect on the court's ideological balance, it would have tended to reinforce the court's conservatism. This ideological stability cannot explain the court's precipitate increase in activist policy making. Further evidence that ideology should be disregarded can be found in the Ohio court. Ideology would be an unsatisfactory explanation for the active policy making that the court embraced in economic cases and its decidedly restrained approach to social issue cases during the first half of the 1980s. The Ohio court during that time had a constant ideological balance, yet it was decidedly activist in making its pro-underdog economic policy while it was decidedly non-activist in making its decisions in social issue cases.

Table 6.1
Partisan Control of Indiana Governmental Branches and the Number of Activist Indiana Supreme Court Decisions, 1981–1990

YEAR	GOVERNOR	CONTROL / HOUSE	CONTROL/ SENATE	ACTIVIST DECISIONS
1981	REPUBLICAN	REPUBLICAN	REPUBLICAN	1
1982	REPUBLICAN	REPUBLICAN	REPUBLICAN	0
1983	REPUBLICAN	REPUBLICAN	REPUBLICAN	0
1984	REPUBLICAN	REPUBLICAN	REPUBLICAN	1
1985	REPUBLICAN	REPUBLICAN	REPUBLICAN	1
1986	**REPUBLICAN**	**REPUBLICAN**	**REPUBLICAN**	1
1987	**REPUBLICAN**	**REPUBLICAN**	**REPUBLICAN**	1
1988	**REPUBLICAN**	**REPUBLICAN**	**REPUBLICAN**	5
1989	DEMOCRAT	SPLIT	REPUBLICAN	1
1990	DEMOCRAT	SPLIT	REPUBLICAN	2

Information with respect to gridlock is from *Book of the States, 80–81, 82–83, 84–85, 86–87, 88–89, 90–91 editions* (Lexington, Ky.: The Council of State Governments).

THE ACTIVIST ADVOCATE

Table 6.3 describes the presence or absence of the various factors that might have explained activist judicial policy making by the three courts during the periods of their greatest activism. In that table the variables that had some potential effect on any of the three courts are listed in the first column, and their presence and potential effect on active policy making is indicated in the second, third, and fourth columns. None was present during the activism of all three courts and, because their potential was thus limited, none is a necessary concomitant of judicial activism. The exception, of course, is that each of the three courts had a justice who, during the periods of the respective courts activism, was an advocate of judicial policy making. Justices Shepard, Neely, and Celebrezze were each a strong proponent of judicial activism for his court. The apparent difference between the three courts that did not choose the activist role during the 1980s and the Indiana, West Virginia, and Ohio

Table 6.2
Partisan Control of Ohio Governmental Branches and the Number of Activist Ohio Supreme Court Decisions, 1981–1991

YEAR	GOVERNOR	HOUSE	SENATE	ACTIVIST DECISIONS
1981	REPUBLICAN	DEMOCRAT	DEMOCRAT	1
1982	REPUBLICAN	DEMOCRAT	DEMOCRAT	4
1983	**DEMOCRAT**	**DEMOCRAT**	**DEMOCRAT**	8
1984	**DEMOCRAT**	**DEMOCRAT**	**DEMOCRAT**	5
1985	DEMOCRAT	DEMOCRAT	REPUBLICAN	2
1986	DEMOCRAT	DEMOCRAT	REPUBLICAN	2
1987	DEMOCRAT	DEMOCRAT	REPUBLICAN	0
1988	DEMOCRAT	DEMOCRAT	REPUBLICAN	1
1989	DEMOCRAT	DEMOCRAT	REPUBLICAN	0
1990	DEMOCRAT	DEMOCRAT	REPUBLICAN	0
1991	REPUBLICAN	DEMOCRAT	REPUBLICAN	3

Information with respect to gridlock is from *Book of the States, 80–81, 82–83, 84–85, 86–87, 88–89, 90–91 editions* (Lexington, Ky.: The Council of State Governments).

courts of the 1970s and 1980s was the presence of these advocates. Justice Shepard joined the Indiana court when its reputation, within and without Indiana, was low. He wanted his court to regain or exceed the eminence that he had discovered in its history and he identified the failure of the court to make policy as an important cause of its diminished stature. Justice Shepard saw judicial activism as the means by which the Indiana court could return to prominence. In his many and varied nonjudicial published articles he did not circumscribe the limits of acceptable judicial activism and his activist decisions on the Indiana court were wide ranging, from tort doctrinal innovation to utility rate making. Justice Shepard's educational background, political experience, and publication record set him off from his fellow justices and qualified him as the court's leader, which made his advocacy credible. This leadership together with his written advocacy gave judicial activism a legitimacy that it did not have prior to his appointment to the court.

Table 6.3
Influence of Factors that had a Potential Effect on the Level of Judicial Activism

VARIABLE	W.VA. 1977-86	OHIO 1981-86	IND. 1986-90
Docket Control	P	A	A
Int. App. Ct.	A	P	P
Merit System	A	A	P
Elective System	P	P	A
Gridlock	A	P*	P*
Dem. Majority (Court)	P	P	A
Rep. Majority (Court)	A	A	P
One Party Court	P	A	A
Divided Court	A	P	P
ACTIVIST ADVOCATE	**P**	**P**	**P**

P means the factor is present.
A means the factor is absent.
* In at least one of the activist years.
Information with respect to gridlock is from *Book of the States, 76–77, 78–79, 80–81, 82–83, 84–85, 86–87, 88–89, 90–91 editions* (Lexington, Ky.: The Council of State Governments).

Justice Neely's attachment to judicial activism seems to have had its origin with his policy interests and his confidence in the correctness of his conclusions. He observed that "the advantage which I brought to the . . . judicial scene was that I had the perspective of both an economist and politician rather than a lawyer."[11] Unlike the apparent universal span of Justice Shepard's acceptable judicial activism, Justice Neely endorsed judicial policy making only within rather narrow borders. His approval of judicial activism extended only to its use in those areas of the law that he believed were unable to excite the interest and gain the attention of the legislature and the executive. The activist decisions he made on the court were, correspondingly, more circumscribed than Shepard's and were generally confined to tort doctrinal innovation. Justice Neely's leadership of his court was clearly intellectual rather than social or personal. Neely's recognized intellectual brilliance, his organized, systematic but selective advocacy of judicial policy making, and his innovation of policy-making decisions prior to the election of 1976 were his contributions to the policy-making explosion of the post-1976 election West Virginia court. Although the liberal Democratic court majority that was elected in 1976 carried activist decision making beyond the bounds of Neely's acceptance, the earlier activist decisions he reached on the court from 1973 to 1977, prior to the election of the liberal Democratic majority, together with his published advocacy of his activist philosophy and the popular acceptance that his books have received, established judicial activism as a legitimate, though not universally accepted, judicial role. This role was embraced by the post-1976 justices in their transcendent active policy making.

Justice Celebrezze's advocacy was not, intrinsically, of judicial activism but rather was of specific substantive decisions that were coincidentally activist. His judicial decision making was driven by his political goal of being governor of Ohio and by the pervasive, but unstated agenda that would advance that goal. The range of his activist decisions was truncated not, as with that of Justice Neely, by the confines of a philosophy of activism but rather by a gubernatorial platform that counted economic activism an advantage but social activism a detriment. Judicial activism was legitimate if it facilitated, but not if it detracted from, the formation of a political coalition within the Ohio Democratic Party. Unlike Justices Shepard and Neely, Justice Celebrezze did not have the advantage of a legal education at a prestigious national law school and he did not reveal any interest in judicial activism aside from its product. His relevant education was in the Democratic precincts and wards of his native Cleveland, Ohio, and his interest was gubernatorial nomination rather than judicial activism. He was interested in the political ramifications of his decisions and this political concern made him the leader of "his" court, the majority of which was of Democratic justices. After Celebrezze's defeat in the 1986 judicial election, activism continued in the post-1986 Ohio court, at a lower, but still significant, level without his leadership. The post-1986 court was decidedly bi-polar, with the Democratic judges reaching activist decisions and three of the four Republican justices continuing the traditional non-active course. Regardless, it is clear that the legitimacy that partisan political judicial activism had achieved under the leadership of Chief Justice Celebrezze survived its master in some form, at least with the court's Democratic judges. The addition of activist decisions in social issues cases to the economic issues cases that were the limit of the Celebrezze court's activism may have signaled a change from judicial activism motivated by political ambition to motivation by ideology. Chief Justice Celebrezze interrupted the Ohio court's traditional jurisprudential repose to serve his political purpose and mustered a majority from his fellow Democratic justices for activist decisions in economic issues cases. The genie of judicial activism, once freed from its master's political bottle, expanded to serve the ideological preferences of the subsequent Court's majority. The influence of Frank Celebrezze's activist advocacy on the Ohio court survived his defeat and continued as an attribute of the Ohio court, perhaps to await a new activist advocate.

COMPARISON OF THREE ADVOCACIES

There were three distinctly different philosophical bases for the activism advocated for the 1980s courts in Indiana, West Virginia, and Ohio: abstract or activism for activism's sake, ideological or activism driven by attitude, and pragmatic or activism in service of political goals. Abstract activism was advocated by Justices Shepard and Neely of the Indiana and West Virginia courts, respectively. They advocated an active role for their courts in governmental policy making without regard for the ideological direction of the result. There was no necessary correlation between the advocates' ideology and their court's resulting activist decisions. Ideological activism is exemplified by the post-1986 Ohio court ; it was a more utilitarian judicial activism, serving the policy preferences of the court's majority. The post-1986 Ohio court's brand of ideological activism was earlier exhibited by the postwar California court and the Michigan court of the 1960s and 1970s. This activist philosophy advocates judicial activism when it serves the court's preferred ideology; for the California and Michigan courts it was liberal policy[12] and in post-1986 Ohio it was moderate liberalism. Ideally, the collective attitude of the court's majority and this ideological activism would be perfectly correlated.[13] The third manifestation of judicial activism was pragmatic activism that supported the partisan political goals of the court's members. Devotees of this variety of activism would embrace activism, whether the direction of the decision was liberal or conservative, that furthered the majority's political goals, but would eschew activism if its expression threatened them. This third brand was the activism of the 1981–1986 Ohio court. This partisan-based activism would exhibit a substantial, but less than perfect, correlation with the court's ideology because the court's political goals would be expected to be roughly correlated with its ideology.

These manifestations of judicial activism with different philosophical explanations would reasonably have different durations. Activism supported by a philosophy of judicial role might become a permanent attribute of the court. As a court that has traditionally deferred to the state legislature and to its own prior decisions is exposed to advocacy of activism by a justice who believes that the court has a proper role in making policy, it might incorporate policy making as an acceptable judicial pursuit. This role could become institutionalized with continued practice. The New Jersey court in the second half of this century followed this course.[14] The deference of the earlier New Jersey court to the state legislature and to its established common law was interrupted by the introduction of an activist judicial philosophy by the accession of an activist advocate, Justice Vanderbilt, to that court. The adoption of Vanderbilt's activist philosophy and the resulting flow of judicially made policy gradually changed the court's culture and eventually transformed the state's legal culture; this transformations survived the retirements of Vanderbilt and his original disciples. Judicial policy making by the New Jersey court is now an integral part of the state's governing apparatus.[15] The Indiana court may be following in New Jersey's footsteps. This abstract or activism-for-activism's-sake judicial activism is not as likely to experience opposition as the other types. Opponents do not have a powerful popular focus. As long as the court's policy is not made exclusively on one side of the political divide, partisan political leaders would not be offended and would likely reserve their energies for the more immediate, and personally rewarding, contests for electoral gain. Opposition by a legislature or a governor to this politically neutral judicial activism would be unlikely; each would as likely be relieved that the court's activism had eliminated potentially difficult or politically embarrassing decisions that they might have to face as it would be to become actively hostile to the court as an institution. This judicial role might excite opposition by a conservative legal organization, such as the state bar association. However, without help from more involved allies with selfish goals, the opposition of a state bar association is, at best, a voice crying in the wilderness.[16] Because of the lack of substantial opposition this pure judicial activism would have the greatest chance for permanence.

Judicial activism that serves the ideology of the court's majority seems to accurately describe the post-Celebrezze Ohio court. The long-term prospect of such judicial activism would seem to be more precarious. The court's ideology can be reversed if the ideology of the majority changes. It is not unlikely that when the majority is replaced by an insurgent former minority that the new majority would embrace a role of judicial restraint in reaction to its predecessor's activism. Many thought that the Ohio court, after the judicial election of 1986, would reject judicial activism: the newly elected chief justice "underst(ood) that judges are not legislators in robes"; a newly elected associate justice had based his election campaign on opposition to the previous court's attempt to "legislate." However, that court continued to be activist, albeit not on its previous scale. The post-1986 Ohio court was ideologically balanced and continued to play its activist role, now in service to its moderately liberal majority.[17] In this guise, the Ohio court seems to be emulating the U.S. Supreme Court's policy-making role, to make governmental policy consistently with the location of its ideological balance.

The least stable institutional activism would likely be based in its pragmatic service to the political goals of its members. The judicial tenure of a politically ambitious leader is likely to be short-lived; it is likely ended by both success and failure. It is unlikely that an ambitious judge would remain on a court very long without attempting to move to the more attractive higher office, the focus of the justice's ambition. The American Bar Association's Canons of Judicial Ethics, which have been adopted generally by the states, require a judge who becomes a candidate for a nonjudicial office to resign from the bench.[18] Removal of the politically ambitious justice would likely remove the partisan activist advocate. Very few, if any, state high court would have another politically ambitious, potential leader in reserve. Elimination of the ambitious judge's partisan political goal would remove pragmatic activism's *raison d'être*. The Ohio court's activism escaped this precipitate termination when its activist advocate was defeated in 1986 by the fortuitous ideological balance it achieved and that is served, from time to time, by its activist role.

ACTIVIST ADVOCACY IN PERSPECTIVE

Both the three-court and six-court comparisons have spotlighted activist advocacy as an explanation of judicial activism, a factor that has had little attention.[19] None of the variables, other than the presence of the activist advocates, is a potentially necessary influence for a policy-making court. All the others have been absent when at least one of the three courts was activist. These other variables may be sufficient in various combinations to explain judicial activism. For example, the combination of the presence of intermediate appellate courts, political gridlock in the other branches, an elective selection system, and a court that is politically divided with a Democratic majority may be sufficient in combination with an activist advocate. These were present and possibly moved the Ohio court to activism. A unanimous Democratic, elected court with absolute docket control that has an activist advocate was sufficient during the period of the West Virginia court's activism. A politically divided court with a Republican majority and an activist advocate who was selected by a merit system in a state experiencing political gridlock made policy in Indiana during the late 1980s. These very different possibly sufficient combinations of variables in just three courts illustrate the extreme hazard in concluding that any combination of factors is a concomitant of judicial activism generally. However, a comparison of the state courts with and without an advocate of active policy making clearly leads to the conclusion that an advocate of judicial policy making is a very important, probably necessary component of judicial policy making in state supreme courts.

The three activist courts were led to activist decision making by a judge who was determined that his court would make policy by its decisions. This should not be misunderstood to suggest that an activist advocate assures that a court will decide each case it considers in an activist manner. It does not. The Ohio court, when it was most active, refused to make the activist decision in the social issue cases. It should not be misunderstood to suggest that the activist advocate will decide to make judicial policy in every case in which it is possible. It does not. Justice Shepard decided against creating a cause of action for a child's loss of its parent's consortium and the Indiana court agreed with him. Nor should it be misunderstood that a court with an activist advocate will always agree with its advocate. A majority of a court may decide to actively make policy in a particular case, although its activist advocate opposes such decision. In West Virginia a majority decided to invalidate the state's public school funding structure, although Justice Neely favored continuation of the legislative plan and registered his disagreement in a dissenting opinion. In Ohio the court overruled the common-law disqualification of a spouse's testimony in criminal trials, although Chief Justice Celebrezze opposed the majority in a strongly worded opinion. These three courts provide strong evidence of the importance of advocacy of judicial policy making. They do not conclusively prove that activist leadership is a sufficient or necessary condition for judicial policy making in all courts, at all times, and in all kinds of cases, but they clearly indicate that activist advocacy must be accounted for in any consideration of the determinants of judicial assumption of a policy-making role.

The effect of an activist leader on a court is to legitimate the activist decision, to make it an acceptable alternative role for the other judges if the activist decision represents the majority's preference. Activist advocacy is a stimulus that impacts the first part of a judge's two-part decision-making process. It makes judicial activism an acceptable alternative to deference to the state legislature or to judicially established doctrine.

NOTES

1. *Blankenship v. Cincinnati Milicron Chemicals, Inc.,* 433 N.E.2d 572 (1982).

2. *Pittsburgh Elevator Company v. Board of Regents,* Case No. 15438, decided June 30, 1983.

3. *Dearborn Fabricating and Engineering Corp., Inc. v. Wickham,* 551 N.E.2d 1135 (1970).

4. *Heath v. Church's Fried Chicken, Inc., et al.,* 546 A.2d 1120 (1988).

5. Student note, "Rebuilding the Wall of Sovereign Immunity: Municipal Liability for Negligent Building Inspection," *University of Florida Law Review* 37 (1986): 343, 371.

6. *Blackburn v. State Farm Mutual, Inc.,* 697 P.2d 425 (1985).

7. The elimination of these factors is the result of the application of the comparative method, specifically, the absence of covariation of the dependent variable, judicial activism, and the particular factor. For a full consideration of the application of the comparative method to different political systems, see John P. Frendreis, "Explanation of Variation and Detection of Covariation," *Political Studies* 16 (No. 2, 1983): 255–272.

8. Justice Robert Holmes.

9. Justice Blanche Krupansky. Because she served on a court with six other justices, all of whom had participated in a general election for their seats and, more significantly, because she was regularly part of the minority Republican bloc that ineffectually opposed the early 1980's Court's activism, her non-election would have had no significant effect on the court's activism.

10. *Book of the States, 76–77, 78–79, 80–81, 82–83, 84–85, 86–87 editions* (Lexington, Ky.: The Council of State Governments).

11. The Hon. Richard Neely, *How Courts Govern America* (New Haven: Yale University Press, 1981).

12. Lawrence Baum "State Supreme Courts Activism and Accountability," in *The State of the States*, Carl Van Horn, ed. (Washington, D.C.: CQ Press, 1989) p. 108.

13. This kind of state court judicial activism is similar to the judicial decision making by the Supreme Court. See Segal and Spaeth, *The Supreme Court.*

14. G. Alan Tarr and Mary Cornelia Porter, *State Supreme Courts in State and Nation* (New Haven: Yale University Press, 1989).

15. Tarr and Porter, *State Supreme Courts*.

16. In the 1986 Ohio chief justice election the Ohio Bar Association opposed the reelection of Frank Celebrezze because of alleged "improper behavior" but the "muscle" of the opposition campaign came from groups of potential tort defendants whose funding "fueled massive campaigns." Baum, "State Supreme Courts," at p. 125.

17. In 1987 that majority was H. Brown, Locher, Sweeney, and Douglas. In 1989, Resnick replaced Locher.

18. Canon 7(A)(3), Canons of Judicial Ethics of the American Bar Association.

19. Tarr and Porter discussed the importance that the presence of Justices Vanderbilt, Heflin, and Traynor of the New Jersey, Alabama, and California courts, respectively, had in certain changes that occurred in their courts. Tarr and Porter, *State Supreme Courts*.

Bibliographic Essay

There have been few studies of activism in state supreme courts. The first modern look at the phenomenon attempted to discover a relationship between a justice's activist decision and the justice's political philosophy. Because of the coincidence, at the time these studies were made, of activist decisions and liberalism, the expectation was that activism and liberalism were significantly related. Glick and Vines determined the preferred judicial role of the justices of four state supreme courts and tested this expectation with each justice's judicial decisions. They concluded that the relationship between a justice's ideology and the justice's preferred role was not clear. Henry Robert Glick and Kenneth N. Vines, "Law Making in the State Judiciary: A Comparative Study of the Judicial Role in Four States," *Polity* 2 (1969): 142. Wold reached the same conclusion as a result of his study of activism in four different state supreme courts. John T. Wold, "Political Orientations, Social Backgrounds and Role perceptions of State Supreme Court Judges," *Western Political Quarterly* 27 (1974): 239. Baum and Canon directed their focus to the court as a unit and concluded that activist state supreme courts were driven by "a general activist tradition" and the coincidence of liberal justices and a possible liberal decision. Lawrence Baum and Bradley Canon, "State Supreme Courts as Activists: New Doctrine in the Law of Torts," *State Supreme Courts, Policy Makers in the Federal System*, Mary Porter and G. Alan Tarr, eds. (Westport, Conn.: Greenwood Press, 1982). Baum narrowed his focus to tort doctrinal development and civil liberties cases and concluded that activist decision making was associated with a court's liberal ideology. One recent study examined state supreme court decision making in public school finance cases and, significantly, found that a court's activism and its ideology had independent effects. William Swinford, "A Predictive Model of Decision making in State Supreme Courts," *American Politics Quarterly* 19 (1991): 336.

Most interest in judicial activism has been focused on the U.S. Supreme Court because of the prominence of its policy-making decisions during the past seventy years. Canon does a thorough job of summarizing the resulting literature in Bradley Canon, "A Framework for the Analysis of Judicial Activism," *Supreme Court Activism and Restraint*, Stephen C. Halpern and Charles M. Lamb, eds.

(Lexington, Mass.: Lexington Books, 1982). The Halpern and Lamb book is a valuable compendium of studies of different aspects of the sometimes elusive concept of judicial activism.

Index

About the Author

CHARLES S. LOPEMAN is Assistant Professor of Political Science at the State University of West Georgia. Prior to his career in teaching, Professor Lopeman served as a practicing attorney and government official.

ISBN 0-275-96455-8

HARDCOVER BAR CODE